call mother a lonely field

call mother

a lonely field

LIAM CARSON

First published 2010 by
HAG'S HEAD PRESS
www.hagsheadpress.com

Every effort has been made to trace and contact copyright
holders before publication. If notified, the publisher will
rectify any errors or omissions at the earliest opportunity.

10 9 8 7 6 5 4 3 2 1

ISBN 978-0-9551264-5-1

Set in 12pt on 16pt Jensen
Printed in the UK by MPG Books Ltd, Bodmin, Cornwall

for Niamh and Eithne
grá go deo

And like young Irishmen in English bars
The song of home betrays us
                                    —Jackie Leven

1
TEARMANN
sanctuary

My father would often tell me his dark dreams. In them, I am always a little boy, and we are lost in a forest. It is night, and we cannot see where we are going. I fall into quicksand, I am trapped, I am sinking. My Da frantically tries to rescue me. He stretches his hand to me, but cannot reach me. After his death, my own dark dreams came.

I see myself sitting on the Black Mountain, gazing down on the city. Immediately behind the Black Mountain rises the summit of Divis Mountain, whose name comes from the Irish *dubh ais* or black place. I look out to Belfast Lough and there is a massive swell building near Helen's Bay. A huge wave rises, a wall of sea rising like a dragon from the depths, a tsunami that will drown the whole of Belfast. And although I am on the mountain, I can also see into the kitchen in Mooreland as if it is only a couple of feet away. My Ma and Da are sitting down to tea, oblivious to the catastrophe hurtling towards them. I run down the hillside, but I know it is too late, I know I cannot save them.

I find my dream echoed in an old *scéal sí*, or fairy tale, from Donegal, called *Na Trí Thonnaí*—the three waves. It tells of a man and his son out fishing on the open sea. It is a quiet, calm day. Then three large waves rise behind them as they head for land. The first is big, the second larger, and the third is so massive, they fear they are about to be drowned. The father asks his son to cast a knife *ins an tuath*. Into the *tuath*—a word that is difficult to translate. In Dinneen's dictionary, it is defined as evoking the sinister: 'wrongness, goety or negative magic'.

The son does his father's bidding, hurling the knife into the heart of the demonic wave. Within the blink of an eye, the wave vanishes, and the men come safely to land. That night the son is visited by a man who tells him the knife is embedded in his daughter's forehead—and that he must accompany him to remove the knife. He is taken to a fairy island and warned to refuse anything he is offered. He is brought to where the girl is stretched on a bed; he removes the knife, and she arises, safe and sound. The island people offer him all manner of things, but he refuses their gifts. The man tells the son he must forsake his native land. And so he does, heading for America, never to see his father again.

For my father, Liam Mac Carráin, Irish was a place of refuge. He was once interviewed for BBC Radio Ulster's *Tearmann*—where guests were asked what gave them sanctuary in their lives. He chose the Irish language itself. He hid within and took comfort from words.

He arrived into this world as William Carson on 14 April 1916, only ten days before the Easter Rising. He spent his childhood *i dteach bheag i sráid bheag*—in a little house in a little street, not far from Clonard Monastery, just off the Lower Falls Road. There was one room downstairs, two upstairs, and an outdoor toilet. His father, Davy Carson, was a fitter for Harland and Wolff—but he lost that job on 21 July 1920, when he was forced out of the shipyard in an anti-Catholic and anti-socialist pogrom.

A contemporary account tells of the fear on that day:

> The gates were smashed down with sledges, the vests and shirts of those at work were torn open to see if the men were wearing any Catholic emblems, and woe betide the man who was. One man was set upon, thrown into the dock, had to swim the Musgrave channel and, having been pelted with rivets, had to swim two or three miles, to emerge in streams of blood and rush to the police officer in a nude state.

My grandfather was lucky to escape a beating or worse. In the next few days, seven Catholics and six Protestants were shot dead in the conflict that spread throughout the city. In the period between July 1920 and June 1922, over 20,000 Catholics were driven from their homes; 9,000 men were forced out of their jobs; and nearly 500 people were killed in sectarian attacks in Belfast.

Davy Carson never regained a full-time job. For years he struggled to make ends meet. He would get temporary jobs from time to time—*obair chrua mhaslach*, as my father described it—heavy, taxing work with a spade or pick in hand, often in the cruellest of weather. But as the 1920s drew to a close, and the depression of the 1930s loomed, the building work dried up. In 1928, he teamed up with some friends; they bought ladders, cloths and buckets, and set themselves up as window cleaners. It wasn't easy to make a living at first. Most of the local women could only afford to pay a few pennies, and even the pennies were hard to come by, money was that tight for the people of the Falls. But soon he was cleaning windows for the local shop-keepers, for offices, and even the local police station.

One day the nun who ran the girls' workhouse at the corner of Dunmore Street asked my grandfather to clean their windows. He was delighted—this was a large building with lots of windows, and he reckoned he'd get a decent payment, at least ten shillings. When he had the windows all spick-and-span, the nun asked him how many of a family he had. Five children, so a family of seven in total, he told her. The nun handed him a bag in which there were seven holy medals, seven scapulars and seven copies of the *Agnus Dei*.

'Now,' she said, opening the door for my grandfather, 'there you go. A medal for each and every one of you. Thanks very much and God bless you.'

'Reverend Sister,' he replied, 'I don't want to be disrespectful to these holy things—but I've a wife and five children to feed. I don't know any shopkeeper who'll take these instead of money.'

The nun's face reddened with shame. 'Oh my, I'm so sorry, I didn't think about that.' She handed over a pound. 'I hope that's enough. Come back next month and every month after that.'

Davy Carson was also a great man for the music. He had a fine voice and knew a lot of traditional songs, although he only had the one in Irish—'Fáinne Geal an Lae' or 'The Dawning of the Day'. As well as being a good singer, he could play the fiddle and the tin-whistle.

My great-grandfather was also called William Carson, and was a Protestant. He 'turned' Catholic when he married his second wife. Apparently, he was an Orangeman, and came from Ballymena. My father told us how his forebear had nine children with his first wife. After her death, he fell in love with a girl who worked for him. She consented to marry him, but on the condition he convert to Catholicism, and move to Belfast. There he had a further thirteen children: he fathered the equivalent of two soccer teams. He attended mass every morning, and the exposition of the Blessed Sacrament every afternoon.

In my mind's eye I imagine him at his doorway in the evenings, calling his children home. He ticks their names off on a roll, one by one. At night they all crowd into the house—or, actually, two little Belfast two-up-two-downs knocked into one. But it is all speculation. He died even before his last son, my grandfather, was born.

In his later years, my Da would often recall his father and there was hardly a day he wouldn't think about him. He described him as the smartest man he ever knew. Not that he was particularly educated—the only schooling he had was from his time in Barrack Street Primary School, and from library books. But there was little he couldn't turn his hand to. Quite apart from his skills as a fitter, he was a right jack of all trades—sewing, shoemaking, tailoring, painting, cooking. The family didn't need to buy toys, my grandfather made them himself—toy boats, trains and trucks, wooden horses and the like for the boys; dolls, baskets and prams for the girls. Neither did the family have any need for a cobbler or a tailor: he mended the shoes himself, and made all the family's clothes.

My father recalled that the older folk thought a child born after the death of its father had healing powers. My grandfather was said to have such powers. He had cures for whooping cough, thrush and other throat infections. In his youth, he practised his healing when asked, even though he didn't actually believe in it himself. To 'cure' thrush, he would blow three times into the affected child's mouth, invoking the Trinity. For whooping cough, a lock of his hair would be tied to the shirt of the sick person. He would comment, my father said, that he would sometimes be left nearly bald, and would never go out without his cap.

There were even superstitions and magic beliefs that lasted into my Da's time. He wrote of the Belfast lamplighter, who would emerge at twilight to illuminate the city. He carried a long pole from which dangled a lit wick encased in a mesh. The Falls' girls stood beneath the gas lamps with their dresses stretched out before them, believing they would be filled with gold. As soon as they looked down, the gold vanished like a will-o'-the-wisp.

If he lacked any real healing powers, my grandfather was a great man for stories, and therein lay his true magic. He would tell my Da stories of ghosts and of the fairy folk, of knights and of the great warriors of Irish mythology, Cú Chulainn and Fionn Mac Cumhaill. He wove tales about historical heroes he admired—Thomas Russell, Jemmy Hope and Wolfe Tone. He would take my Da and his brother Pat to McArt's Fort on Cave Hill, and tell them how Tone founded the United Irishmen at the very spot where they stood.

They would have journeyed to Cave Hill by tram. For my Da, trams were always special. *Meallacach* is the word he used— beguiling, alluring, enchanting. He imagined that he must have first boarded a tram in his father's arms when only a baby. He remembered being taken on tram trips from the age of about four. Up the stairs they would go, to the upper deck of one of the old red and cream trams that were common in Belfast. He loved hanging over the rail, the wind blowing in his face, his father holding him in a firm grip. Every weekend for years, my Da and Pat would join their father on journeys to the outskirts of the city—Greencastle, Dundonald, Castlereagh, the banks of the Lagan.

The trams were gradually phased out, replaced by electric trolleybuses. The tracks were pulled up from the tram routes, one by one, but the overhead cables remained. The trolleybuses would last until the 1960s, and I can remember them myself. My father hated them. He was still living in O'Neill Street when the trams were taken from the Falls. Eventually, all the trams vanished. When he boarded the last tram from Ardoyne Depot, his heart was broken.

My father was young when his father died suddenly. He had called on my Da to get up for work one morning. When my Da came back at the end of the day, his father was dead. He was distraught that he hadn't had a chance to say goodbye, or to receive his father's farewell blessing.

In later years he began to dream about his father. For over twenty years he had the same dream nearly every night. He is standing at the corner of Clonard Street and the Falls Road, waiting for a bus. Instead of a bus, there arrives a tram. He lights up with delight when he sees it. Just as he is about to board, the tram picks up speed, and disappears into a mist. No matter how many times he had the dream, he never managed to board the tram.

Why he should have this dream so often puzzled my father. For the life of him, he couldn't figure it out. Finally he decided to visit a doctor friend who knew a bit about psychology. He told him of his childhood tram journeys. 'The tram and your father are inextricably linked. That tram is an image or symbol of your father. You can't get on that tram, and you never will, no matter how many times you have the dream.'

In 1930, at the age of fourteen, my Da started work as a post office motorcycle messenger, delivering telegrams to insurance brokers and shipping companies throughout the city. Each

morning the messengers lined up before an inspector, who refused to let his men start their work unless the buttons on their uniforms were sparkling. He earned twelve shillings and seven pence a week. He followed in a family tradition—his grandfather and three uncles worked in the General Post Office. He would give his mother ten shillings, which paid for rent and coal. The remainder covered his expenses—a packet of ten Woodbine at two pence, a tram journey out of town for a penny.

In his book *Is Cuimhin Liom an t-Am (I Remember the Time)* he described his awakening to the beauty of Irish. In the post office, he met Ruairi Ó Maolchallan and Padaí Ó hÉigeartaigh. He found himself spellbound listening to their Irish—*faoi dhraíocht acu ag comhrá le chéile i nGaeilge*. But in a different story my father

15

told me of a political discussion he had at work, where a colleague shamed him by asking how he could possibly call himself an Irish nationalist if he couldn't even speak his own language. Whatever the impetus, he determined to master the language as quickly as possible, and attended two classes a week. He practised his Irish at socials in An Cumann Gaelach, where he would meet migrant mill-workers, girls from the Donegal *Gaeltacht*. After two years, he went for the *Fáinne* test of proficiency in Irish. There was a silver *fáinne* for moderate ability, and a gold one for complete fluency. He was examined by Domhnall Ó Grianna, brother of famed Donegal writers Seamus Ó Grianna and Seosamh Mac Grianna. His examination was short and sweet—Domhnall simply stated, '*Bhfuel, a Liaim, tá tú ann.*' (Well, Liam, you're here.) '*Tá,*' replied my father, whereupon Domhnall removed his own gold *fáinne* and pinned it on my father's lapel. He was already famous for his outstanding command of Irish.

In May 1934, my father went on his first visit to Rann na Feirste, birthplace of the Ó Grianna brothers—renowned for its many outstanding poets, singers and storytellers. Amongst their number was Johnny Shéamaisín, with whom my father stayed. Johnny's house was nothing less than a treasure store of language and literature, both oral and written. Johnny's family had a huge collection of books in Irish, as his brother Niall worked for the publishing house of An Gúm. My father would spend hours in the family library, thumbing through book after book. Every night after supper, they would decamp to the house of *seanchaí* Micí Sheáin Néill, often listening to stories until three in the morning.

My father learnt much from these people. Theirs was a world where social contact was based on *ag áirneáil*—friendly night visits to nearby houses—where singing and storytelling were the prime forms of entertainment. Beauty and precision in speech was profoundly valued. My father moulded himself in their image, to such an extent that in later years, he would come to be praised by many as a wonderful folklorist and storyteller. As a teacher of Irish, he valued and promoted the 'direct method', emphasising listening and speaking.

In his visits to Donegal, he was fulfilling a dream of the great writer Seosamh Mac Grianna—who welcomed an injection of new life into the Donegal *Gaeltacht* by urban lovers of Irish from Belfast. Mac Grianna despised the in-between world of the small town, which he believed all too easily succumbed to the tide of English. In his essay 'Galar na Gaeltachta' ('The Disease of the *Gaeltacht*'), published in *An tUltach* in December 1924, he expanded on his theme.

Mac Grianna wrote with a deep sorrow of what he saw as the spiritual death of his own people in their gradual embrace of all things English, *Gallda*. He envisioned the salvation of Irish within literature. Until the age of sixteen, he hadn't spoken a word of English himself; the language was never uttered in his family's house. By the time he was at college, he was winning prizes for the excellence of his English. Mac Grianna tells us he immersed himself in English books. He read and reread the English canon, he drank in its poetry and its mindset. Just as he learnt English in this manner, so he thinks Irish should be taught: the starting point had to be literature. The soul of a language is in its literature, not in grammar lessons. He wonders how many Belfast and Dublin people understand that in the *Gaeltacht* language and being are one and the same. Without knowing the rules of Gaelic poetry, how can one get to grips with the race that created it? Do they know that the business of 'introductions' is alien to Donegal people?

My father read many classics in Irish first, not in English: for a period An Gúm churned out translations of popular novels, *Captain Blood*, *Ivanhoe* and *Ben-Hur* and the like. Amongst the publisher's army of paid-by-the-word translators was Seosamh Mac Grianna, who produced an acclaimed version of Joseph Conrad's *Alymayer's Folly*, rendered in Irish as *Díth Céille Almayer*. At the core of Mac Grianna's own work is a solitary man entering the heart of darkness. He visits the bleak storm-lashed mining towns of Wales in *Mo Bhealach Féin*. A simple translation of the title would be 'My Own Way' or 'My Own Path'. Dinneen's dictionary, though, points to the complex weave of meanings in *bealach*. Not only is it a way, road or path, but also a mountain pass; an old or disused road; an inlet; a passage. The lexicographer goes on to tell us that *bealach* is quite different from *bóthar*, another word for a road; a *bóthar* has fences and limits a *bealach* need not have.

Mac Grianna's own *Dá mBíodh Ruball ar an Éan (If the Bird Had a Tail)* might have been the definitive novel of modern urban Ireland had it been completed. As it stands, it is a strange work, full of political and moral intrigue. He evokes a demi-monde of corruption, nascent fascism, lies, morally corrupt artists, the dark end of the street of 1930s Dublin writ large. But the book leads nowhere, and becomes a puzzle. Where was he taking us? For Mac Grianna himself, there was just a dead end. The book's final words are heartbreaking:

Thráigh an tobar sa tsamhradh, 1935. Ní scríobhfaidh mé níos mó. Rinne mé mo dhícheall agus is cuma liom.

The well ran dry in the summer of 1935. I will write no more. I did my best and I don't care.

Mac Grianna simply gave up the ghost, or rather, became a ghost of himself. The proud Gael, the ambitious genius, the brave republican, fell apart. During the 1940s and 1950s, Mac Grianna frequently moved lodgings. In Fairview, not far from where I now live in Dublin, he was called 'Butts'. People saw him reduced to smoking cigarettes picked from the gutter. His wife Margaret, or Peggy, killed herself in 1959. His son Fionn drowned the same year, and suicide was suspected.

Writer Proinsias Mac an Bheatha raised a fund for Mac Grianna, and regular payments were made until he was placed in St Conal's Psychiatric Hospital in Letterkenny, where he spent his last thirty-one years, dying in June 1990.

It was rumoured that Mac Grianna did, in his later years, actually give the bird a tail, and also that he had written a novel in English. There are letters from his wife that survive, where she refers to him as Joe Greene. One of Mac Grianna's last letters to An Gúm was in English, surely a gesture of utter contempt, and was a request for payment. He concludes the letter by recalling a verse that he learnt as a 'very small, precocious boy':

> *With empty hands I will rise to meet Him*
> *Meekly thus in the shape of His cross;*
> *And the Lord, who made them so frail and feeble*
> *Maybe will pity their strife and loss.*

Seoṁaṁ Mac Ṡmanna

Tá Seoṁaṁ Mac Ṡmanna cinn i láčaip na h-uaiṗe agus ní copáil go mbeið ṗé ṡḃaice aon peiṗḃneoiṗeacc a ḃéaṁaṁ aṗiṡ. Iṡ miṁceaṁac an cṗuaiš ó an ṗóḃál ṗeo. Ní ġan ḃṗéiṡ ṿo ṗáṗuiġ Seoṁaṁ aon peiṗḃneoiṗ Ṡaeilge eile a ḃí čuaṗ ṫe'n a ṫinn i ṿcaca ṫe ġlaine ṗéile agus ḃuaiṿ cumpaṁṫeacca ṿe. Tá ṗóṡra ṿá ṗoilṗiú againn ṗa leačanač eile ó čoiṗce aca cuṗca aṗ ṿun ṫe ṗóṁéince aiṗ. 'Sé cuṗṗóiṗ aca ṗóṁṗa oiṗeaṿ aiṗṡṗ́o a ḃailiú, máṗ ṗéiḃṗi ṫeo ó, a'ṡ a ḃéaṗṗaṗ aṁáin ṿo'n peiṗḃneoiṗ cinn. Cáṗ ionann a'ṗ an cṗian aṁ i ṁ-Ḃṗinn nuaiṗ a ḃí an Ṡaeilṡ agus na caoiṗṡ Ṡaeiṿealača i ḃṗeiṁ ní cuṡṗaṗ aon čočá ó'n Ṡcác ṿo peiṗḃneoiṗí nó luče ealaṿan aca cinn nó pó-aoṗca ṫe leaṁṗcaṁ

ṿá ṡceiṗo. Tá an "Oiḃí Liṗe Ṗeaṗṗon" aṡ i Ṡaṗaṁ.

Tá ṗúil againn go ḃṗpeaṡṗóčaṗ áṗ léiṫeoiṗí an ġaiṗm čaḃṗac ṗeo. Ḃa aṗ "An c-Ulcač" a čéaṿ-čoiṗṡ Seoṁaṁ-Mac Ṡmanna a' peiṗḃnaṿ: ḃí ṗé aṗ ṿuine ṿe'ṗ na peiṗḃneoiṗí óṡa a ṗo'ṗṗeaṡaṗṗ Uoṗo ṗiann an eṡaṡaiṗc úi ṁuiṗeaḃaiṡ. Ḃa aṗ an ṗáiṗéaṗ ṗeo a ṗoilṗiṡo ṿe'n čéaṿ uaiṗ ḃunóṗ "Uóčaṗcač Ṿuiḃlionnač," "An Spáṗ agus an Ṡṁuaiṁ" aguṗ "Ṗili ġan

loṁṗáṿ." Ḃa máiṫ ṫinn iaṗṗaṿ aṗ áṗ léiṫeoiṗí cuiṿiú go ṗáil ṫeiṗ an iaṗṗace ṗeo. Ní ḃeiṿ ċóṡáil a ġcinn aṡ luce ṗáoṗaiṡe aguṗ láče ná Ṡaeilge má ċeiṗeaṁ aṗ áčċuinge aguṗ cuṗṗóiṗ an čoiṗce ṗeo. Láḃṗaṿ Ṡaeióil Ulaṿ an ḃeaṡ-ṗoṁṗla čṗé ṗinčiṗéal a čuṗ čuiṡ an Ciṗčeoiṗ:—

Ciṗce Seoṁaṁ Mac Ṡmanna,
F./C. Kevany ⁊ Son,
1, 2, 3, Spáro an Feiṗṡṡe,
Ḃaile Áča Cliaṫ.

Sníteaṁ na h-Uiṗcí-
mianṁaí iṗ ṗeaṁṁ aṡ
cóṁluċc eiṗne
i
ṡcluain eoiṗ
Ḃain Cṗial áṗ áṗ ṡCuiṿ
ᴘoṡaince

Clólann Chromaic, 45 Sraid Mhic Amhlaoidh. Béal Feirsde.

2
TAIBHSE
revelation

My father started teaching Irish in the mid-1930s. He was standing at his front door when he noticed two men putting up a poster across the street, reading *Conradh na Gaeilge, Craobh Uí Chruadhlaoich—Cumann Chluain Ard*. Curious, he approached the men, addressing them in Irish. They replied in English, explaining that they had just begun learning Irish, and that they were about to establish classes. But they needed teachers, and asked if he would help. A week later he held his first class. Such was the demand for Irish that classes were held on three nights of the week for adults, and a children's class on Sunday mornings. On Tuesday nights, English was completely forbidden in order to encourage the students to use as much Irish as possible. There were lectures and debates, quizzes, and, of course, storytelling.

From the 1930s on, Irish spread throughout the city. In 1942, when Conradh na Gaeilge celebrated its fiftieth anniversary,

Belfast was host to many events—in halls and clubs, but also in the streets and parks. My father gave a series of open-air classes at the bandstand in the Falls Park. In 1943, a young woman called Mary Maginn came to my father's class. She adored Irish and learnt it rapidly. My father often used to joke that my mother badgered him for extra private classes to 'study the irregular verbs', a suggestion she dismissed. 'God forgive you, Liam, I never did!' Whatever the truth, they fell in love, and after walking out with each other for a year, married on the Feast of the Holy Cross in 1944.

Their wedding vows were in Irish.

Pósaim thú leis an fháinne seo, tugaim duit an t-airgead agus an t-ór seo agus bronnaim ort mo mhaoin shaolta.

I wed you with this ring, I give you this silver and this gold and I bestow on you all my worldly goods.

It was a vow my father took quite literally and quite seriously. In later years my mother's knuckles bulged, wrinkled skin grew over the ring, and she had to go to hospital to have it cut off. My father bought her a new ring, etched with a leaf and flower pattern.

'Daddy gave me everything, he never took a penny for himself, just some money for cigarettes and a few books.' I am nineteen years old, and am hunkered on the rug in front of the fire in our living room. Sitting at my mother's knee. Drinking coffee and smoking a cigarette, I listen to her as she takes me on a journey through the past. I am coming down from a nasty trip; it is a Saturday night in summer, and the Da is at Cumann Chluain Ard with his cronies. He'll drink a few beers or a few glasses of wine or port. Tell stories, joke, gossip: it is his weekly night out.

On this night I've already ventured to Musgrave Park with friends, and taken far too many magic mushrooms. I get the horrors, hallucinations. In the Roadhouse Inn, I watch snooker players transmogrify into ape-men; the carpet turns into waves, the floor wobbles. I melt into a land where time stands still. Every second is endless. I arrive home, frightening my mother. She thinks somebody has broken into the house. I rush to my bedroom, where I tear my clothes off—I am drenched in sweat. Swarms of flies buzz in my brain; I close my eyes, and see writhing masses of snakes.

My mother knows something is wrong, and comes up to the loft. 'My God, have you been taking drugs?' I tell her exactly what I'm on and that I don't feel well. I wait for a burst of anger, but she simply takes me down to the living room, covers me with a blanket, and makes me a cup of coffee. Then she begins to talk. 'They used to murder each other down the Loney on a Saturday night, all the men's money went on drink.' Her father's alcoholism had made her loathe drink. And God forbid that she should marry a man like her father. Years later, I heard the story of what happened a few weeks after her wedding day. My father and a friend were coming home one night, both a little tipsy. As my Da took out his keys, my mother leaned out the upstairs window and emptied a bucket of water over both him and his pal—who turned out to be Father Joe McBrearty, an old school friend of my father's, just returned from the missions.

'People respect your father. He knows a lot. He's a good man.' For the first time I see she is actually proud of her husband. My Da comes back home from his night out, smiling and flushed after his few jars. He is baffled.

'What's going on here?' he asks.

'Ach, never mind, sure I'll tell you tomorrow,' says the Ma. After my night of nightmare, she has brought me back to reality, back to home, back to time passing.

The next morning my Da is more curious than upset. '*An bhfaca tú taibhsí?*' he asks. Did you see ghosts? *Taibhse*—a ghost, a phantom, a revelation.

The only ghosts I have glimpsed are those of my folks' past. A world of drunken bar brawls on Saturday nights. A world of scarcity, of outdoor toilets, cramped terraces, pawnbrokers. A family of ten in a two-bedroom house was not unusual. A world where children worked as 'half-timers' in the mills—they'd work from six to nine in the morning, and then go straight to school.

A world haunted by the shadow of the workhouse.

During the 1970s, my mother went to night classes in St Joseph's, studying English. Her first essay was 'My First Day at Work', and I still have it. It is written in her gorgeous copper-plate script—and has some punctuation, a rare thing for the Ma. Her writing was usually a breathless torrent, no full stops, no commas, no pause in the urgency. She opens by telling the reader that her mother died when she was only seven years old, when her sister Annie was only two-and-a-half. After her mother's death, she is taken care of by an aunt. Then when she reaches fourteen, her aunt takes ill. My mother leaves school to look after the house. Shortly after, the aunt dies, and my mother has to work in Greaves' Mill.

She becomes a doffer, 'collecting bobbins that were filled with yarn from the machines stacking them in wooden boxes and refilling the machines with empty ones'. She feels 'cold and fearsome at the sight of the huge mill and the crowds flocking through its doors their chattering voices breaking the stillness of the morning'. Her head throbs with the incessant din of the mill; the building is full of dust; her back aches from constant bending and lifting. She describes herself as looking like a character from *Jane Eyre*. Her dress 'consisted of short brown coat, brown shoes and ankle socks, my hair which was long was plaited and tied with a bow'. She wonders how anybody could employ somebody with 'such a timid and childish figure as I must have projected to them'. Her spirits lift when she is brought into a 'jolly crowd' for lunch, but she goes home dreading that this job is her fate.

and childish figure as I must have
projected to them. I was soon awakened
out of my thoughts by the harsh voice of
a man, "Well what is your name and
your age", feebly I found my voice and
answered, he looked up and seemed to
peer through me then he called one of
his assistants a young girl, gave her a
piece of the paper and told her to bring
me along to the overseer of the room
where I was to work.

In *Is Cuimhin Liom an t-Am*, my father quotes a doffer's song:

> *You'll easy know a doffer*
> *When she comes into town*
> *With her long yellow hair*
> *And her ringlets hanging down*
> *And her apron tied before her*
> *And her pickers in her hand;*
> *You'll easy know a doffer*
> *For she always gets a man.*

My mother, I think, dreamt of escape with a terrible passion. In my father, she found a man who shared her unswerving devotion—a good man, a moral man of few vices. Together they dreamed of a world different from their past. They would give their children the Irish language, a tongue that represented something different. Irish and the home were fused together. My father could quote Blake, and would sometimes sing 'Jerusalem'. He dreamed of an Ireland that was a 'green and pleasant land' like Blake's Arcadian England. Together, my Ma and Da set out to create a home that would be a microcosm of the kingdom they wanted to see.

3
TEACH *house*

My parents spent their honeymoon in Dublin, a weekend in the North Star Hotel in Amiens Street, just opposite Connolly Station. They enjoyed those two days. Free State food was good, compared to the rationed fare in the North, and they made sure they ate well. When they returned to Belfast, they went to live in Linden Street, renting two upstairs rooms. It was impossible to rent a whole house, and buying one was simply out of the question. The money wasn't there. Life was hard enough. Their cooking facilities consisted of a single gas ring and an open fire. They had to go downstairs to fetch water and coal. Despite these inconveniences, they were happy. My father's mother lived nearby, in 3 O'Neill Street, and proved to be a great help when their first child, Caitlín, was born in 1945.

About this time, my father was delivering letters in Divis Street, where estate agent Tomás MacArtáin had an office. Tomás was an Irish speaker, and he and my father became firm friends. Finally, my Da asked if Tomás could get him a house to rent. Tomás thought for a few seconds, then mentioned a house in Raglan Street. The tenant had just died, and people were approaching him, making bids for the key—a common practice in those days, one which made him uneasy. He gave the key to my Da, saying, 'Go and take a look at the house anyway, and if you like it, it's yours.'

The house was filthy and 'through-other', as my mother might say. The fireplace covered in mounds of soot, the wall-paper peeling. No matter, it was a house, my father thought. It could be fixed up. He rushed home to tell his wife. She was delighted, impatient to see their new home. The Da managed to dissuade her until the place was spick-and-span. A painter pal, Liam Ó Maoláin, re-papered the walls, painted all the doors and windows, cleaned the chimney. He only charged my father the price of the materials. My Ma and Da were proud of 'tigh s'againne'—our house, a place they felt was theirs. The Irish for inside or in is istigh (is tigh)—in the house, within. And a teach is also a region or a kingdom.

My parents were Falls people, with all that that entailed. Catholic people. Nationalist people. They belonged to a partic-ular world with particular values. They had a framework that made sense of the world for them. In the ritual of the mass they were bound to their neighbours, to the world, to God. In the incense, the statues, the Stations of the Cross, the rosary, the stained glass, the Latin, they reached a form of communion and community that held up their daily lives. In this world the dead passed through a veil, simply gone ahead to another place where they waited behind the veil for their families and their friends. My Da believed this. One afternoon he told me if he'd been born in Iran, he would have been a devout Muslim. Perhaps it was not so important to be a Catholic as it was to *believe*.

My father was intensely religious. He carried his rosary beads everywhere. One fine summer's day, he was delivering post on the Shankill Road. He was walking down Fortengale Street, where Billy Moore, the Grand Master of the Defenders of Ulster Lodge Number 796, lived. Outside his house, there was a group of Orangemen, dressed in their full paraphernalia: black bowler hats, dark blue suits and orange sashes. They were waiting with their banner and big drum for Billy to come out. The Da had a letter for Billy, and knocked on the door. Billy opened the door and said, 'Ach Wullie, come on in and have a drink.' My father was known on the Shankill as 'Wullie' and it never occurred to them that a Catholic might be delivering letters there on the Twelfth of July, the day it happened to be. They knocked back a few bottles of McCaffrey's Ale together. 'Now, Wullie,' said Billy, 'sing us a song, I've heard you know a lot of Orange songs.' Which was true. My father loved them, and knew many of them had Irish tunes—'The Boyne Water' was a version of 'Rosc Catha na Mumhan'; 'The Protestant Boys' went to the tune of 'Lillibulero'. The Da started off with 'Dolly's Brae':

> Come all ye blind-led Papists, wherever that ye be,
> Never bow down to priest or Pope, for them they will disown;
> Never bow down to images, for God you must adore,
> Come, join our Orange heroes, and cry 'Dolly's Brae no more.'

After another beer and a whiskey, my father was in full flow. As he was opening another bottle, he spilt some ale on his shirt. He put his hand in his pocket to get his handkerchief, and pulled out his rosary beads, which fell to the floor. Billy looked at the Da with shock. 'Ach, you ould deceitful Papist,' he said, 'you never let on to me that you kicked with the wrong foot.' So now the people of the Shankill knew my father was a Fenian, but they continued to be as friendly to him as they had ever been, and would often call on him to sing a song.

The Falls was a thriving shopping district in the 1940s— there were shops of every kind—clothes and shoe shops; butchers, fishmongers and bookmakers; and pawnshops with their three brass balls above the doorway. A lot of the shopkeepers came from Omeath, which was still a *Gaeltacht* in the 1930s. The Ó Maolchraoibhe family had a fishmongers beside The Clonard Cinema; Eoghan Ó Fearáin had a vegetable shop; and Peadar Mac Con Midhe had another vegetable shop in Castle Street. They all spoke naturally fluent Irish. In his book, my father recalls how the Omeath people were known as 'Fadgies' on the Falls. He could never understand why, until he began to learn Irish himself. Peadar Ó Mearthaile—a post office inspector who had relations in Omeath—explained the origins of the nickname. About a hundred years ago, he said, there was a big Omeath crowd living in Marquis Street, none of whom had any English. Many of them were named 'Paidí', and in the bars Belfast people would eavesdrop on their conversations. Of course they didn't understand a word, but they would hear them saying *'A Phaidí, a Phaidí', 'Maise, a Phaidí', 'Leoga, a Phaidí'* and so on. Hence the 'Fadgies'.

The first person who founded an antique bookshop in Belfast's Smithfield Market was a little chap from Omeath. When a fellow dealer had business to attend to with him, he would say, *'Tá mé ag gabáil go bhfeice mé an fear beag fá leabharthaí.'* (I'm going to see the wee man about books—'The Wee Falorie Man' of folk song repute.)

> *I am the wee falorie man*
> *A rattling, roving Irishman,*
> *I can do all that ever you can*
> *For I am the wee falorie man.*
>
> *I have a sister Mary Ann*
> *She washes her face in the frying pan,*

And out she goes to hunt for a man
I have a sister Mary Ann.

I am a good old working man,
Each day I carry a wee tin can
A large penny bap and a clipe of ham
I am a good old working man.

My father loved reading books in Irish. In the days before television, he would read a book a day. He was a member of the Falls Road Library, and his ticket allowed him to take out a book a week. This, of course, was hardly enough to satisfy his hunger. So along with the book he was officially borrowing, my Da would also smuggle another two or three, hidden inside his overcoat. He wasn't stealing them, and fully intended to bring them back. But the days turned into weeks, and the weeks into months, and it wasn't long before he had a collection of well over a hundred unofficially 'borrowed' books.

From time to time, his conscience would nag at him. After a few of years living in Raglan Street, the family was making ready to move house.

'What about those books?' said my mother. 'Isn't it high time you brought them back to the library?'

'How on earth am I going to do that now? Sure, the librarian will know I took the books, and I'll only end up in trouble with the law. We'll take them with us. I can sneak one or two back every now and again.'

There was a local library not far from the new house in

Mooreland, so my Da stopped going to the Falls Library. The books remained in a tea chest. Then the missionaries came to the new parish church, St Agnes's. My Da attended every service. One evening the seventh commandment was the subject of the sermon—the preacher telling the congregation that those who took that which did not belong to them would never be forgiven if they did not return the stolen goods to their rightful owner. My father slept little that night, and the very next morning he packed three large parcels of books, put used stamps on them and wrote the library's address on them. He then put on his post office uniform and waited until a Royal Mail van passed the top of the street. And so the books were returned.

Shortly after, the assistant librarian left his job to open a shop in Castle Street. One day the Da dropped in to buy a book, and started to chat with the former librarian, Declan. He confessed to the ruse that he'd come up with to return the books. 'So it was you. We all thought it was Father McCagney from Clonard Monastery. He was forever looking for religious books and books in Irish, so we assumed he must have been the culprit.'

My family still has a copy of the January 1950 issue of *An tUltach*. The magazine is in the old Gaelic script, and uses the old spellings. On the front page, there is a photo of my mother with my sister Caitlín and brother Ciaran, who's only a toddler. The Carsons are 'family of the month'. The article tells how Caitlín 'has a few words of English that she learnt from children in the street but she only speaks Irish at home'. The author laments the fact that Ciaran will have to learn English at school—but proceeds to remark that, while it may not be unusual to hear adults in Belfast speaking Irish, it is wondrous to hear it in the mouths of children. The author wonders if 'this land will ever change', and says that English is a 'cause for sadness' in our lives. Here is my family in the days before I was born, urban pioneers urging the renewal of a language and a spirit.

4
TÍR NA N-ÓG
land of youth

Leaving Raglan Street behind, my parents lit out for the new territory of suburbia. For years, they had scrimped and saved—and in 1953, with the help of a credit union loan, they bought their own house. 3 Mooreland Drive, Andersonstown.

Mooreland was a small 1950s estate, a place where families shared in a new suburban vision. For the first time in their lives they had bathrooms, indoor toilets, things thought unimaginable. The world was brightening.

Mooreland was a place for young parents—and a paradise for a child, there were that many playmates. Here my Ma and Da found a house designed for life, a place they would not leave until 1995. Here I was brought up and spoke Irish.

Our Irish was house Irish, home Irish, an Irish of the heart. It was a language that felt warm. At Holy Child Primary School, I was regarded as a curiosity, an exotic eccentric nicknamed

'Fluent'. The other boys would poke and provoke me—'Go on then, Fluent, say something in Irish. How do you say fuck?'

Growing up in 1920s Lowell, Massachusetts, Jack Kerouac knew his language set him apart. Of French-Canadian descent, his family spoke a variety of Québec French called *Joual*. Kerouac attended the Saint Louis de France Parochial School, where pupils would pledge allegiance to *la race Canadienne Française*. He only started speaking English at the age of six, and he recalled the day when 'door' entered his mind—his first English word.

In March 2009, the Americas Society in New York hosted a panel discussion with the title 'Jack Kerouac: An Unlikely Franco-American Writer'—exploring what author Mark Abley described as 'a bilingual identity that for much of his life Kerouac chose to hide'. The discussion featured a contribution from Joyce Johnson, who recalled Kerouac's 'shame of being a Canuck', but also how he 'murmured' to her cat in French. Another speaker was journalist Gabriel Anctil, the author of articles in the Montreal newspaper

Le Devoir, which revealed the existence of two unpublished works Kerouac wrote in French. In one of them, 'La Nuit est ma Femme', Kerouac wrote about a *malaise identitaire*, an illness of identity.

> I am French Canadian, brought to the world in New England. When I am angry, I often swear in French. When I dream I often dream in French. When I cry I always cry in French. I never had a language to myself. French patois up to six, and after that the English of the neighbourhood boys. And after that, the grand forms, the great expressions of the poet, the philosopher, the prophet. With all that today I am all mixed up…

The only other people in Mooreland who spoke Irish were the Bradys—the real thing, from the Donegal *Gaeltacht*. As a child, I played with Kevin Brady, later to be murdered by loyalist madman Michael Stone at a republican funeral in Milltown Cemetery. His own funeral was to be the occasion of further horror.

I was born on the 22nd of February 1962, only seventeen years after the end of the Second World War. My mother still had unused ration books for powdered milk and eggs. We even had a gas mask and an air-raid warden's helmet. My mother would talk about the Belfast Blitz, when hundreds of Luftwaffe bombers laid waste to the city. She recalled how the people of the Falls fled to the safety of the Black Mountain. There they watched the city in flames. The seemingly endless waves of bombs turned the night sky into an incandescence that shone brighter than day.

By 1962, the Cold War had replaced the Nazi threat. Rosaries were said for the conversion of Russia. A few weeks before I was born, USA spy pilot Gary Powers had been released in Berlin. In the Kremlin, Khruschev—Stalin's immediate successor—was in power. On the day of my birth, John F. Kennedy had announced plans to land men on the moon and the space race had begun.

CEATHRAR
ASTRANÁT
AG SIÚL AR
AN AER

Is féidir do aon duine buachan . . . aon am . . . aon áit.
Triail d'ádh le teicéad no cuid de thicéad. Is furasta an
triail . . . agus féach an duifear a dhéanfadh buachan.

IRISH SWEEPS DERBY SWEEPSTAKE

AN IOMAD CEAD-DUAISEANNA   **£50,000**

CRANNCHUR NA hÉIREANN, DROICHEAD NA DÓTHRA, BAILE
ÁTHA CLIATH, 4
OIFIGÍ I gCORCAIGH, SLIGEACH AGUS AG 9-11 SR. GRAFTON, BAILE ÁTHA
CLIATH, 2.

TICÉID £1 AN CEANN

DATA DEIRIDH 27 BEALTAINE

CAPS

Mooreland is immediately adjacent to the North's biggest GAA ground, Casement Park, named after Irish patriot and anti-imperialist, Sir Roger Casement. My family's move coincided with the ground's opening. The August 1953 issue of *An tUltach* reported an occasion that was as much religious and political as it was sporting. The Milltown band played 'Faith of Our Fathers'. Cardinal Dalton spoke in English and in Irish, telling the crowds that Casement Park was an embodiment of patriotism, of loyalty to the traditions of the Irish race, and a testament to the indestructible spirit of the nation. Soil from Croke Park was mixed with the soil of Casement Park, showing what *An tUltach* described (using non-standard spelling) as '*an aontacht do-scartha eadar tuaisceart agus dusceart na tíre seo*' (the unbreakable bond between the north and south of this country). Dalton spoke of Roger Casement, of his courage in defying the might of the British Empire. Until such time as Casement's remains were released from Pentonville Prison and allowed a proper funeral in his native land, the park would be his lasting memorial, an example to the youth of the country.

The house in Mooreland felt big to me as a boy. I had dreams and waking nightmares of obliteration and annihilation. When there was thunder and lightning, I would try to find the place in the house where I felt safe, where nothing could touch me. I would squeeze into the gas meter space under the stairs. Above the door, there was a little wooden ledge. There, for many years, I kept a model howitzer cannon; a spring lever allowed you to fire bits of broken matchstick. As I crouched, I imagined the sky as huge white egg cracking open, the heavens opening in an explosion of blinding light. And then time itself froze into a terrifying silence. In my sleep, I dreamt of nothingness, a void of brilliant white, shimmering into eternity. It was a nothing in which no matter how far you went, you were still in nothingness, with nothing eternally before you.

On Sundays, crowds would flood the streets. Casement Park was also the Falls Road trolleybus terminus. We lay at the outer edge of the city, where new streets and open fields adjoined each other. My brother Pat wandered through the wilderness of Colin Glen, climbing trees, scrambling through bushes, collecting birds' eggs. He would carefully prick the eggs with a pin, blow and suck on the holes until the eggs were hollow. Then the eggs were gently packed in sawdust, kept in biscuit tins. Collecting was an obsession that possessed us. Cards from sweet cigarette packs. Stamps. Coins. Matchboxes. Beer mats.

In the Dump—a small patch of wasteland running between Mooreland Park and Stockman's Lane—my friends and I built a den. A trench was excavated, lined with old carpeting, roofed with corrugated metal, a hole forming an improvised chimney. We roasted spuds in a fire, their skins all sooty. I would head home late in the evening, my face smoky and warm. There were dens everywhere—in Casement Park, deep in the overgrowth between the banks and the ground's walls; in the briar jungle between the MI motorway and Musgrave Park Hospital. Anywhere secretive.

There's a Robert Crumb cartoon where we see the changes over time in an American small town. A few shacks in the middle of a pastoral Eden; then comes the town hall and the sheriff's office; a decade later the railroad comes to town; then tram lines and telegraph cables appear. Buildings fall into disrepair, are demolished.

So it was with Andersonstown. Mooreland Park runs parallel with Stockman's Lane, home to 1930s houses and ex-servicemen's cottages. The largest house in the lane belonged to writer and actor Joe Tomelty for many years. Joe was famed throughout Belfast as the writer of the hugely popular BBC radio sitcom *The McCooeys*. He appeared in films such as John Huston's *Moby Dick*, and Carol Reed's *Odd Man Out*, a haunting noir tale of an IRA gunman on the run in a snowbound Belfast. Joe's house later became a shelter for down-and-outs, and my mother was a volunteer there. It had stables, and an orchard.

In Andersonstown, there were the remnants of the original leafy suburb on the edge of the countryside. Not far from Mooreland was the local lawn tennis and bowling club, and the big houses and long gardens of Fruithill Park and the Andersonstown Road; behind Owenvarragh Park, there was still an open field through which flowed the stream that gave its name to the street—*abhainn bharra*, the river of the staves, which then becomes the Blackstaff River at Stockman's Lane.

At the age of six I played with my friends in the Dohertys' front garden, where we created a childish simulacrum of our immediate world. We fashioned a little suburb. A bush became a shop. We took on the roles of mammies and daddies, with jobs, duties and responsibilities.

We even had a car—a magnificent machine built by Seánie Doherty. Seán was older than us, and a mix between Pied Piper and resident mad scientist. He seemed to more or less live in the family coal-shed, his laboratory. Here he spent most of his free time surrounded by electric bric-a-brac—batteries, wires, spark plugs, circuit boards, bulbs, bits of televisions and radios. In his hands the average Belfast 'guider' (an improvised go-kart)—became an imitation Model T Ford. He even used a proper car seat and steering wheel. There were working lights, and a real horn that beeped.

Our domain extended from Mooreland into the neighbouring areas of Stockman's and Owenvarragh. In the 'Mushroom'—a little mushroom-shaped cul-de-sac off Stockman's Lane—we climbed the electricity pylon. We'd roll up scraps of newspaper and smoke them. We enthusiastically ate chewing gum scraped from the pavement, drank rainwater from rusted railings. Our parents would make us packed lunches of jam sandwiches, crisps, apples and orange juice when we headed off on one of our expeditions. We packed our ex-Army issue schoolbags with notebooks, pens, torches. And off we'd go to explore the local storm-drain system. We'd slip on our wellies and walk along the Owenvarragh River, vanishing into the murk of the storm drain. After a hundred yards you came to a metal grille that blocked you from going any farther. But there was a ledge, where we would sit and picnic.

In my early childhood, my closest friend was Declan Mc Cavana. Our houses were barely fifty feet from each other. Our favourite reading included *The Book of Inventions* by Leonard De Vries. Its introduction promised a 'voyage of discovery', in which readers were encouraged to undertake 'amazing scientific experiments… performed with simple, everyday things that can be found in almost every household'. Declan and I made a telephone from string and tin cans. In the evening, Declan sat in his bathroom, while I knelt on my bed, leaning out the window, and we'd chat by phone.

On television we loved *The Undersea World of Jacques Cousteau*, where Cousteau's crew constantly overcame adversity ('Today the *Calypso* was attacked by a giant squid. Unfortunately, five of our crew died... but as you know, life on the *Calypso* must go on,' became an in-joke of ours). In various ways, we re-enacted the Second World War, its presence still potent in the popular imagination. In the 1960s, British comics—the *Victor*, the *Hotspur*, the *Commando* series—were full of brave Brits in battle with nasty Nazis. We'd buy Airfix models of Stukas, Hurricanes, Spitfires, Messerschmitts; using thread, we suspended them from our bedroom ceilings in mock dog-fight scenarios. We played with Action Men. You could buy different uniforms for them—a British commando, an American GI, a German infantryman, a Free French Resistance fighter. The Ma and Da fully indulged me in my Action Man obsession. The Da gave them names—Frank and Joe Harris, two American GIs (they could never be British soldiers)—and spun yarns about their heroic battles against the Japanese in the Pacific. The two brothers were always saving each other. In winter, the Ma knitted them jumpers and scarves to keep them warm.

What Declan and I—and most of the kids in Mooreland— also had in common was our parents' devotion to the Church. They wanted to see us believe as they did, to see that prayer worked. They sought to shelter us in their faith. In Declan's house I would often be roped into the family rosary. One night I hallucinated, and saw the Virgin staring through the window at me. At mass I drifted on waves of song and incense.

Strength and protection may His Passion be;
O blessed Jesus, hear and answer me!
Deep in Thy wounds, Lord, hide and shelter me,
So shall I never, never part from Thee.

My mother was small, like my father. She was strong. Her arms were muscular. On sunny days she would feed wet clothes through the mangle, turning the hand crank. She baked apple cakes and haystacks—buns covered in honey and coconut. On winter mornings she made my Shredded Wheat with warm milk. She was always in movement, walking, scrubbing, hoovering, painting. In the late afternoon she would sit in a deckchair with a newspaper and nod off. She invested all she had in us, her children. Ever fearful for us, ever wanting to protect. In company she would shuffle slightly, shyly, from foot to foot.

It is nearing October again; it is nearly my mother's birthday, a time when I will always think of her. I remember autumnal walks with my mother and father. Down Mooreland Park, then Stockman's Lane, past Musgrave Park. Over to the Lagan, and along the towpath to Stranmillis, or sometimes up the Black Mountain, stopping at Hannahstown graveyard, down the Springfield Road, Belfast a carpet of gold and brown in the mellow light.

I remember a particular walk on the Lisburn Road, heading into town. It is after Sunday dinner. The light already seems to be fading. Opposite Drumglass Park—where I can still remember the swings being tied up on a Sunday—an old woman approaches us. Would we join her for a cup of tea? She's lonely and hasn't spoken to another soul for days on end. And so we enter the gloom of her house. Peeling patterned wallpaper. The smell of age and abandonment. She makes a pot of tea and serves us biscuits. She brings us into the hallway to show us pictures of her husband. He died many years ago. The photographs show him in the full dress uniform of a British soldier. Her children have grown up, and she rarely hears from them now. Her face is whiskery, crumbed, and she wears layers of clothes. We stay for hours, the Ma and Da listening to her story. As she sits and talks, she is framed by light from her living-room window, growing dimmer as time passes. We emerge into twilight, the streets awash with rain sparkling in the car headlights. As we leave, the Da tells her he will remember her in his prayers. She asks us to call again. And so we do. Over the next year, every few months, we will call in to see her, to see how she's keeping. One day she is simply not there, there is no answer to our knocking. We peer through the windows, the letter box. There is only darkness and silence. My father makes enquiries of the neighbours, and is told she is dead. The house lies empty for years after, decaying, crumbling.

The Da takes Breandán and I to see the Twelfth. We sit on the stairs at the side of a shop, and watch *Na Fir Bhuí*—the Orangemen—and their bands marching along the Lisburn Road, heading for the field at Finaghy. He waves to work colleagues he recognises, and they smile or wave back. Throughout his life my father had numerous Protestant friends whom he held in high esteem. They were men who shared his values—traditional men, family men, Christian men. In Caitlín's I find an old Bible given as a present to the Da. It is inscribed: 'Although we are Catholic and Protestant, we share in the salvation of the Blood of the Lamb. To my brother in Christ.' My Da revered Winston Churchill as a great Englishman, and loved his oratory, the speeches that could stir people's hearts.

On Saturday mornings we'd often go to Belfast City Cemetery, and the Da would make us origami boats that we'd set sail in the fountain. As the municipal graveyard, those buried there were mostly Protestant. Their graves had urns, angels; the paths were straight—the huge cemetery swept up the length of the Whiterock Road. From it, you had commanding views across the city, over to the Lisburn Road. At the height of the Troubles, few Protestants were prepared to go up the Falls. The solution was Cemetery Sunday, a day on which people travelled all over the city to visit the graves of loved ones. The flowers were piled high at the graveyard gates.

Sometimes the Da brought me to loyalist Sandy Row,

where I'd get a lucky bag, sweets or a comic. Sandy Row was renowned for its shoe shops, sweet shops and toy shops. It was also home to the largest tobacco factory in the world, Gallaher's. The business was incorporated on 28 March 1896 to 'carry on in all their branches the businesses of tobacco, cigar, cigarettes and snuff manufacture'.

My father introduced me to these streets and they belonged to him as much as they did to any Protestant. We would admire the decorations for the Twelfth, the red-white-and-blue bunting. There was a huge ceremonial Orange arch, supported by two crenellated towers. It was topped by a representation of William of Orange—King Billy himself, sword held high.

The arch displayed a range of loyal-order symbols—a pentacle embodying friendship and mutual dependency; a coffin, essentially a *memento mori*; a three-branched candlestick not altogether unlike a Jewish *menorah*, representing the Holy Trinity. Curiously enough, there is a Jewish synagogue in Sandy's Row in London's East End. Originally a Huguenot chapel, it was acquired by Dutch Ashkenazai Jews in 1867. Mostly working men, many of them were fruit traders or cigar makers. To this day, the synagogue's interior is orange, a reminder of its Dutch origins.

Saturday nights, the Da took Breandán and myself to York Street Station, down by the docks. Here the trains arrived from the Larne boat, loaded with mail from England, Scotland, Wales, beyond. We'd help my father carry postbags to the Royal Mail vans. In the 1970s, York Street Station was still an old-world place, a final vestige of Victorian Belfast. In the bar—aged wood panelling, stained-glass windows—old men would down pints of Guinness and scan the pages of *Ireland's Saturday Night* and the

Belfast Telegraph. We drank cokes and ate crisps; the Da would have a smoke and a pint. Outside the ferries lay docked along Donegall Quay, the cranes looming over the Lagan. I remember *an clapsholas*, the gloaming, the evening turning to nightfall in Belfast. Huge clouds of starlings would spiral around the river's bridges. Sweeping down to the water's surface, swooping under their arches, and then hurtling up again. Above Donegall Square, pigeons flocked to the parapets of the City Hall and the department stores of Royal Avenue. A cacophony of bird-screech rising above the dim roar of evening traffic.

I remember one blazing Saturday afternoon in July. I am walking with my father, down the few remaining streets of Belfast's Sailortown. The Da is sweating. We go into York Street Station to cool down. By the ticket office, there is a glass case, and inside it there is a model of an old steam train; its side is cut open, exposing the intricate workings of the engine. My father gives me an old penny to put in the slot, the pistons jerk into action, the wheels turn, magical, hypnotic. I am entranced.

On Tuesdays I'd accompany my father to Clonard Monastery for the Men's Confraternity. I remember us on the way up Clonard Street, a man lighting the last gas street lamp in the city. I remember evenings, the Black Mountain darkening over Belfast. I remember the smell of damp clothes after rain. Clonard was huge: candles lit everywhere, incense. A decade of the rosary would be recited. A Redemptorist would preach. The men would sing in unison:

> *Be Thou my breast-plate, my sword for the fight;*
> *Be Thou my armour, and be Thou my might.*

Thou my soul's shelter, and Thou my high tower:
Raise Thou me Heavenward, O Power of my power.

I feel the rasp of my father's beard. I am five years old. He rubs his chin against my soft boy's cheek and tells me one day I'll have stubble like him, that one day I'll also need to shave. It is bedtime. He doesn't read me stories. He doesn't need to. Like his father before him, the Da is an expert storyteller, a walking book. What he reads, he remembers, and what he doesn't remember, he makes up as he goes along. Interspersed with his stories of Irish heroes, there were his own creations—including Koffeedoff:

Koffeedoff had a very bad cough and a very bad cough had he
But he got well when he got the smell from the top of his
     lollipop tree.

The BBC television mast that topped the Black Mountain was the lollipop tree, my father told us.

The stories that moved me the most were those of sorrow and exile, of those who could not return to their home, those who were banished. The story of Colm Cille's return to Ireland from his self-imposed exile in Iona I found unbearably sad. As an act of repentance for his sins Colm Cille had taken an oath never to set foot on Irish soil again, never to look at the beauty of the land and of its people again. When he attended the Convention at Drum Ceatt, he arrived with sods of Scottish soil under his feet, and was blindfolded.

The stories contained worlds nullified by the passage of time. Oisín returns from Tír na n-Óg. Once he touches Irish soil, he ages centuries on the spot. Saint Patrick tells him that his time is gone forever. The Fianna ride out no more. They have even been forgotten, or people merely think the Fianna were a myth, that they never really existed. Oisín's world—his friends, his gods, his beliefs, his codes—is no more.

In the story of the Children of Lir, Lir's evil second wife transforms his beloved children into swans. A curse that will last 900 years. For 300 years they live in a lake near Lir, who visits them daily to tell them of his love, but they then must spend a further 300 years in the Straits of Moyle. They leave, never to see their father again. As they fly to Inish Glora for the final phase of their curse, they pass by their father's castle, now a ruin. Eventually they find sanctuary in a little church, with the holy man Mochua. When the curse finally wanes, they age aeons, wrinkle, wither and die. A statue of the Children of Lir is the centrepiece of Dublin's Garden of Remembrance in Parnell Square, and symbolises the rebirth of the Irish nation after 900 years of English tyranny.

The Da also sang to me. 'Henry Joy' was my favourite, this tale of a great man who instilled men with the courage to defy an empire, to fight for liberty, equality and fraternity, only to suffer defeat and be murdered on the gallows.

It was to Cave Hill that Henry Joy McCracken fled in the aftermath of the Battle of Antrim. He found refuge with local gamekeeper David Bodell, whose limestone cottage nestled within the deep woods by Ben Madigan. Henry Joy was in love with one of the gamekeeper's daughters, Mary, whom he had secretly married.

Cathal O'Byrne's *As I Roved Out*, one of my Da's favourite books, contains many wonderful descriptions of and stories about Cave Hill. The caves themselves—five in total—were reputedly man-made, but by whom and for what reason, nobody knows. The third, fourth and fifth caves are linked by a tunnel. They were the perfect hiding place for anyone seeking a safe haven from the law.

'Henry Joy' is a song of faith and friendship; it is also a song of loss and sorrow. It tells the story of Henry Joy and the United Irishmen from the point of view of a young follower from the Glens of Antrim, stirred into action by the sound of fife and drum, and 'the martial tramp of men'. In its final verse, the narrator watches Henry Joy walking to his death, his sister Mary by his side, and it tells of their farewell kiss.

In Belfast town, they built a tree
And the redcoats mustered there
I saw him come as the beat of a drum
Rolled out in the barrack square
He kissed his sister, went aloft
And waved a last good-bye
My God he died, I turned and I cried
They have murdered Henry Joy

What defines the life and death of Henry Joy is love. One of McCracken's workmen, the English calico printer William Thompson, refused to testify against his employer, despite being given 200 lashes. Prior to his execution, McCracken asked to see his minister and friend, the Reverend Sinclair Kelburn. On arriving, he immediately burst into tears, declaring, 'Oh, Harry, you did not know how much I loved you.'

I see Henry Joy perched on the parapet of McArt's Fort with his telescope, watching for British warships plying the waters of Belfast Lough. When the Da reaches the song's sad end, my eyes and cheeks are wet.

5

ALADDIN'S CAVE

From an early age, my Da introduced me to the Aladdin's cave of Smithfield and its bookshops. On Saturdays we'd go 'down the town' to Smithfield Market, where we'd visit Harry Hall's. Hall's seemed to stock every conceivable type of book and magazine. For a while UFO books were all the rage; Erich von Däniken's *Chariots of the Gods* was the most famous of these. There were also Marvel, DC, Warren, and Charlton comics—all the great American imprints.

We entered the market gate as if entering a small walled city, enclosed within the boundaries of Smithfield Square. Once through the gate, we were on the central arcade, light pouring through the glass ceiling. Little alleyways; tunnels of teetering bookshelves—you had to climb ladders to reach the highest shelves; recesses full of bric-a-brac, torches, cutlery, old radios, scratched records, broken alarm clocks; bikes and prams against

the walls. There were Army surplus stores, music shops, jewellers
—and books, books, books.

There were cheap paperback reissues of classic 1930s pulp
authors—including Edgar Rice Burroughs, the creator of Tar-
zan, with his swashbuckling fantasies and 'planetary romances'.
My favourite of these was *A Princess of Mars*; my father bought me
the 1968 edition 'specially adapted for boys and girls' aged between
twelve and fifteen. Even in its truncated and censored form, this
novel cast a spell on me like none other before, and I quickly
devoured the next ten novels in the Martian series. *A Princess of
Mars* opens with Virginian gentleman and former Confederate

soldier John Carter fleeing from 'ferocious Apache warriors'. He seeks shelter in a cave, where he undergoes a mysterious form of astral projection that transports him to Mars. Burroughs's description of the 'irresistible enchantment' that grips Carter as he gazes at Mars is a quite literal imaginative leap from one world to another, from the mundane to the marvellous.

> I closed my eyes, stretched out my arms toward the god of my vocation and felt myself drawn with the suddenness of thought through the trackless immensity of space. There was an instant of extreme cold and utter darkness.

The Mars of Burroughs' imagination is an arid, dying world. Water and air (produced by 'atmosphere factories') are precious resources; the planet is torn apart by war. But even with its divisions, the various warring peoples of Mars share a common language, though Carter's lover Dejah Thoris mentions a different language still spoken 'in the valley of Dor, where the river Iss empties into the lost sea of Korus' as she recalls an ancient Martian civilisation that died as the seas receded. Most of its archives, records and literature were lost as the oceans and cities turned to dust. Burroughs' vision of a decaying world partly inspired Ray Bradbury's *The Martian Chronicles*, where the Martians effectively become ghosts in the face of human colonisation. In the chapter entitled 'And the moon be still as bright', settler Captain Wilder speaks of how mankind will give the Martian mountains new names, but 'somehow the mountains will never sound right to us... the old names are there, somewhere in time, and the mountains were shaped and seen under those names'.

There was also Robert E. Howard's Conan, King Kull and Solomon Kane. Lester Dent's Doc Savage. Maxwell Grant's sinister The Shadow, much given to gunning down criminals to the accompaniment of a demonic laugh, cackling as he recited his mantras 'The weed of crime bears bitter fruit' and 'Who knows what evil lurks in the hearts of men? The Shadow knows.'

Mike Kaluta was the artist of the 1970s DC comic version of The Shadow. His city was an art deco sprawl, with gargoyles, huge windows, tenements, streets washed by rain, trains on tracks high above the streets—he captured all the detail, just as Jack Kerouac spoke of the illumination of 'every pebble and pubblehole in the street'.

In his novel of a spectral childhood in Lowell, *Doctor Sax*, Kerouac wrote of an 'old dumb brown tragedy', as he put it, in buying *The Shadow* magazines at his local candy store. So it was with the places I bought comics. A news stand at the City Hall, the rain dripping down the plastic sheeting covering the magazines and comics, the sky dark and heavy, the burnt aluminium after-smell of a summer storm. In Kathleen's newsagents near Casement, it was always gloomy: an old glass and wood sweet counter, comics and fading magazines suspended from clips in the window. I'd have to go into the street and point to the one I wanted in the window.

After mass, my father brings me here to buy a comic. *Countdown*, full of strip versions of Doctor Who, Thunderbirds and other television science fiction series. 'He's a great wee reader,' says John, who works there. I am chuffed to hear this, deep down I know this is something good to be. A reader.

At night I burrow under my sheets and read *Robinson*

Crusoe by torchlight. At home the Da has a library of sorts, kept in a wooden bookcase in the parlour. There are books in English, Irish and Esperanto. *Fiche Bliain Ag Fás* (*Twenty Years A-Growing*). Bibles of various hues, different versions. The Da's reading and knowledge of books is populist—in a Victorian sense—but eclectic. H.G. Wells, Rudyard Kipling, Sir Arthur Conan Doyle, Robert Service, Oscar Wilde. He eschews anything 'dirty', anything sexually explicit, anything blasphemous. One day he burns the copy of Edna O'Brien's *The Country Girls* that Pat is reading. But my Da is the person who has opened the Pandora's box of literature, and once opened, it cannot be shut. The post-war world gives us a power unimagined by our parents. We are the beneficiaries of the British welfare state—and, more than anything, the 1948 Education Act. Where the Ma and Da left school at fourteen, their children go on to do A-levels, go to college.

I particularly loved Robert E. Howard's Conan, whom I first encountered in the 1970s Marvel comic interpretation. Barry Smith's artwork created a visual universe as much inspired by Alphonse Mucha, Dante Gabriel Rossetti and the Pre-Raphaelites as by Howard's original vision.

'The Tower of the Elephant', which I discovered in issue four of Marvel's *Conan the Barbarian*, particularly moved me. 'Oh Yag-Kosha, is there no end to agony?' declares an alien who has been kept captive in the deepest recesses of a tower, set in a great garden, surrounded by high walls. Like many Howard characters, he is the last of his kind.

Conan wanders through a universe defined by war, plunder and pillage; a world where new rulers, new nations and new gods obliterate older peoples and older cultures. In Smith's vision, a young Conan wanders through a shadow world of shimmering minarets, decaying temples, the embers of lost civilisations.

Howard himself culled much of what he wrote from Celtic sources, and may have read Fiona MacLeod's versions of Gaelic folklore. He claimed the template for Bran Mak Morn was Goll Mac Morna, an ally of Fionn Mac Cumhaill. In 'The Dark Man', set in Connacht and the Scottish islands, Turlogh O'Brien senses 'the waves of humanity that wax and wane', and thinks of the 'pilgrimage from the dark to the dark'.

In 'The Grey God Passes', Howard retold the story of the Battle of Clontarf. Some accounts have it that he actually learnt some Gaelic, though it is never made clear what form of Gaelic he may have come across. He was alternatively attracted to and repelled by things Gaelic or Irish, once declaring:

> I'm not worrying about my Irish past. What has my Celtic blood ever done for me but give me a restless and unstable mind that gives me no rest in anything I do? Damn the Shan Van Vocht, and the ancestors that went to Sassenach gallows for her, and damn the Irish and damn the black Milesian blood in my veins that makes me like drift-wood fighting the waves and gives me no peace or rest waking or sleeping or riding or dreaming or traveling or wooing, drunken or sober, with hunger or slumber on me.

Conan swears by a deity called Crom, a god whose name was still evoked in Kerry until very recently. Crom, declares Conan, 'rules over a sunless place of everlasting mist, which is the land of the dead'. People imagined Howard was a hard man like his hero, Conan, just as many thought Jack Kerouac was Dean Moriarty, the hero of *On the Road*. On hearing that his ailing mother had lapsed into a terminal coma, with only hours to live, Howard typed a poem that borrowed lines from 'The House of Caesar' by Viola Garvin. He then shot himself through the head. He and his mother were buried three days later, 14 June 1936, in a combined funeral. The final poem read:

> *All fled, all done,*
> *So lift me on the pyre—*
> *The feast is over, the lamps expire.*

Comics opened another world for me, one of infinite possibilities, of unfettered imagination. English comics still inhabited a commonplace world—the heroes were soldiers, footballers, policemen or cowboys. American comics were brash, colourful, alive, futuristic. Ordinary men and women became superheroes. A fit of anger would turn the mild-mannered 'milksop' scientist Bruce Banner into the Incredible Hulk. A bite from a radioactive spider transmuted the shy, bookish, bespectacled Peter Parker into the Amazing Spider-Man. Bombarded by 'cosmic rays', Reed Richards and his fellow astronauts became the Fantastic Four—the elastic Mister Fantastic, the Invisible Girl, the Human Torch and the orange-skinned half-man, half-brick Thing.

I loved characters who lived underground. The blind Mole Man in the first issue of *The Fantastic Four*, a villain you simply pitied. Batman in his Bat Cave, surrounded by computers, laboratory equipment and library. A technological Sherlock Holmes. My favourite was The Spirit, created by Will Eisner: noir, utterly of the 1940s—The Spirit was the adopted name of Denny Colt, a private eye who allows people to assume he has been murdered and buried in Wildwood Cemetery in Central City (in effect, New York). There are subway trains, litter-strewn streets, rotting wharves, steamboats, trams, crowded tenements. In the sweltering heat of the summer, children play in the gushing waters of broken fire hydrants. There are peeling posters on walls, overflowing trash cans. At night Colt emerges from his graveyard den to stalk the city's mean streets, an urban gumshoe angel.

Steve Ditko's Dr Strange would reach for infinity from secret sanctuaries. From the cave of his mentor, the Ancient One, his astral form leaps into the clouds over the Himalayas. From his Greenwich Village loft, his metaphysical spirit dives through the wall, leaves his motionless body. Within a small room he enters dimensions of pure shape. He traverses oceans and continents, his freed spirit conquering all of time and space in its silent flight.

Marvel Comics engaged their readers: the editors and writers would invite comments on their stories, what excited the readers, and the letters pages were interactive forums. Fans would respond in droves to the death of a beloved character, such as Spider-Man's girlfriend, Gwen Stacy, killed by the Green Goblin. The process of creating a comic was made plain—the art of plotting, panel break-downs, pencilling, inking, colouring, lettering and final dialogue was explained. The fans would become the next generation of artists.

Every Saturday night, I would meet friends Bernard Brannigan and Gary Peden, and we would draw comics together. Bernard created The Masked Marauder, and drew exactly like Jack Kirby. He loved Kirby's glittering grandeur, his worlds where Thor and the Norse gods lived in space-age cities; where the Silver Surfer, herald of Galactus, the destroyer of worlds, soars through the universe. When the Silver Surfer confronts the Fantastic Four, he betrays Galactus. As punishment he is exiled from his kind, marooned on earth.

Bernard even acquired a duplicator, and we experimented with printing our work. The results were crude, and we never produced the comic we planned. Soon we drifted apart. For years a treasured book of mine was *The Studio*—a lavish coffee-table book about the New York studio comic artists Barry Windsor-Smith (as Smith now called himself), Mike Kaluta, Jeff Jones and Berni Wrightson shared. It was a space full of bric-a-brac, odd statues, books, unfinished drawings, canvasses, jars of brushes and paint. It was the kind of space I dreamt of, huge but with every corner occupied.

As we grew older the Marvel and DC comics became darker, reflecting reality as much as fantasy. In the 1970s Captain America came to doubt his government and became Nomad. The Black Panther confronted armed revolution in his African kingdom. In Marvel's *Unknown Worlds of Science Fiction*, there appeared a version of the Michael Moorcock story 'Behold the Man', in which time traveller Karl Glogauer travels from 1970 to the time of the gospels, only to find that Jesus is a mentally impaired hunchback, incapable of coherent speech. Glogauer then steps into the role of the Jesus we know. His decision leads to his inevitable death on the cross, where he mutters in English, 'It's all a lie, it's all a lie.' Those witnessing the crucifixion think he is saying, 'Eloi, Eloi.'

When I was thirteen, Smithfield Market was destroyed by firebombers. I remember the day, or rather, the day after. I had gone down the town, shopping with the folks. My mother was in a foul humour, and she and my Da were arguing, tense, debating in hushed voices and semi-coded phrases as if I didn't know what was going on. My Da looked agonised; my mother's face was tight with suppressed anger. At the corner of North Street and Royal Avenue, I bolted away from them, down Gresham Street, towards Smithfield. Where the market had been, there was nothing more than a pile of rubble and smouldering ash; pools of blackened water; singed beds and chairs; half-burnt books. It all seemed so small, so diminished. The magical maze was now a grimy square, a void at the heart of the city.

Shortly after my Da's death, my sister Caitlín showed me a poem she'd found among his papers, 'North Street on Saturday Night'.

The shops were all open till ten o'clock
You could get any thing from a nail to a lock,
A bucket, a basin, a poe or a crock
In North Street on Saturday Night.

They'd come from The Shankill, The Markets, The Falls
And pack The Alhambra and Gaiety Halls
For a deuce in The Pit and 4d in The Stalls
In North Street on Saturday Night.

You could buy sugar candy, black lumps, yellow man
Or a clatter of griskins to fry on the pan
And brown or black laces from Oul' Mick McCann
In North Street on Saturday Night.

You'd get elder, black pudding, pigs' feet, brawn or ham
Veal, beef and pork mutton or lamb
And come home tired but happy for a wing on the tram
From North Street on Saturday Night.

O! those days are gone now; we shall see them no more
And I'm now an oul' fellow of six and three score
But I long for the old times—the fine days of yore
And North Street on Saturday Night.

North Street on Saturday Night.

1

The shops were all open till ten o'clock
You could get anything from a nail to a lock,
A bucket, a basin, a poe or a crock
In North Street on Saturday Night.

2

They'd come from The Shankill, The Markets, The Falls
And pack The Alhambra and Gaeity Halls
For a deuce in The Pit and 4^d in The Stalls
In North St., on Saturday Night.

3

You could buy sugar candy, black lumps, yellow man
Or a clatter of griskins to fry on the pan
And ~~go~~ brown or ~~the~~ black laces from Oul' Mick McCann
In North St, on Saturday Night

4

You'd get elder, black pudding, pigs' feet, brawn or ham
Veal, beef and pork mutton or lamb
And come home tired but happy for a wing on the tram
From North St. on Saturday Night.

5

O! those days are now gone; we shall see them no more
And I'm now an Oul' fellow of six and three score
But I long for the old times - the fine days of yore
And North St. on Saturday Night.

6

TODAY IS
DIFFERENT

Where did the storm of the Troubles begin? The editorial of the June 1966 issue of *An tUltach* excoriates Prime Minister Terence O'Neill's call on Catholics to take an 'active part' in the life of the 'province'. The editor's language is measured, but it cannot conceal his anger. It is high time, he says, for someone to tell Mister O'Neill that the patience, the reason and the restraint are all on our side; the provocation, the bad faith and lack of reason all on the other side. Mention is made of the 'Protestant Pope', Ian Paisley. Who, he asks, will rein him in?

My father once bumped into Paisley on Royal Avenue. Or, rather, Paisley quite literally bumped into my father, knocking him off balance. The Da's postbag fell to the ground, spilling its contents. The 'Big Man' immediately bent over to pick up the scattered letters, apologising profusely. According to my father he was the model of decency and good manners.

Nineteen sixty-nine started as a year of hope. In Belfast, the Shaw's Road community was founded—Ireland's first urban *Gaeltacht*. On Easter Sunday, which fell on 6 April that year, the Esperanto Association of Ireland hosted a Congress in Dublin that brought together Esperantists from Britain, Ireland, and farther abroad. Among their number was my father, and in the souvenir photo of the occasion, there he is in the second row from the top, below a woman in a bright coat, just to the right of the window.

In 1937, my father had been introduced to Esperanto by one of his students, Liam Mac Maoláin. Esperanto had attracted many of the leaders of the Easter Rising. At the age of fifteen, Owen Sheehy Skeffington wrote to a local Cavan newspaper, arguing that 'Gaelic' was dead and that 'the study of Esperanto would be more useful to the youth of Ireland'. Peadar Macken, shot dead at Boland's Mill, was a lover of both Irish and Esperanto. On more than one occasion, James Connolly wrote of the necessity for an international language, one that would protect the linguistic identity of 'small communities, speaking different tongues'. There were many links between Irish-language activists and the Esperanto movement. Micheál Mac Liammóir proposed that all Irish schools teach four languages—Irish, English, French and Esperanto.

My father wore the Esperanto green star with pride, beside his *fáinne*. On his postal rounds in town, he would meet Esperanto speakers from all over the world. Once he struck up a friendship with a Chinese man, who sent him an Esperanto edition of *The Thoughts of Chairman Mao*, also known as 'the little red book'. My father returned the favour by sending him the New Testament. Esperanto was popular with the communists in the 1960s. On another occasion, the Da met up with the captain of a Soviet warship that was in Belfast for repairs. The captain invited the Da, my brother Breandán and me for tea in his quarters—and then took us for a guided tour of the ship, letting us sit in the gun emplacements.

But the Da's closet Esperanto friend was a man he never met, a Dutchman called Arie Kuipers. For fifty years they were pen pals. I have a letter that Arie wrote shortly after *Is Cuimhin Liom an t-Am* was published. It is in Irish, typed, with the fadas inserted by hand. It bears the title '*Is Cuimhin Liomsa, Freisin… Beirt chara gan feiceáil a chéile riamh!*' ('I remember also… two friends without ever seeing each other!'). Written in Voorburg in August 1982, five years before Arie's death, he recalls how his and my father's paths crossed.

Voorburg, 11, Lúnasa, 1982.

IS CUIMHIN LIOMSA, FREISIN ...
Beirt chara gan feiceáil a chéile riamh!

Bhí Domhnach ann, agus mé a' siúl a bhaile tar éis an Aifrinn.
Ba chuimhin liomsa, freisin, ar an t-am, daichead bliain is cúig
ó shin, nuair a thosaigh an síor-charadas idir Liam Mac Carráin
(21) in Éirinn agus Arie Kuipers (34) san Ísiltír.
Chuir mé spéis ins an nGaeilge, agus ba é Liam Mac Maoláin
(go ndéanä Dia trócaire ar a anam,,an fear é ó bhfuair mé
an fíor-sheoladh.
De bhrí nach raibh an t-Esperanto ag Liam Mac Carráin,
ná an Ghaeilge agamsa, scríobhaimis ár litreacha i mBéarla
ar dtúis. Ach d'fhogail Liam an t-Esperanto agus theagasc Liam
an Gaeilge domsa. (Agus mé gan síleadh go bhuil bhféidir
aon theanga ann ar talamh níos deachara(do eachtrannaigh)
ná Laidin nó Gréigis!).
Agus 'na bheagán is 'na bheagán ní raibh aon fhocail ann ach amháin
Esperanto agus Gaeilge!
A chara dhílis, bheirim mo buíochas duit ar son do charadas
agus do chomhbhá i laethanta áthasa agus brónacha.
Go mbheannaí Dia duit,, do do ghaolta, agus do do thír ghrádach!

Arie.

(Litir ag leannúint fá leith)

There was one Sunday, and I was walking home from mass. I remember the time, too, when the undying friendship between Liam Mac Carráin (21) in Ireland and Arie Kuipers (34) in the Netherlands started. I was interested in Irish, and it was Liam Mac Maoláin (may God have mercy on his soul) from whom I got the actual address. Because Liam Mac Carráin didn't have Esperanto, nor did I have Irish, we wrote our letters in English at the start. (And me not realising there might be a language more difficult for foreigners to learn than Latin or Greek!) Little by little, soon there were no words other than those in Esperanto and Irish! My true friend, I give thanks to you for your friendship and sympathy through days of joy and of sorrow. May God bless you, your relatives, and your beloved country!

Arie.

If Arie and the Da never met, at least they did get to hear each other's voices in the 1970s, when they would send cassette letters to each other. Our family has a photograph of Arie, where he is part of a large gathering seated for tea. He seems to be listening to somebody, and has a hint of a grin. In his right hand he appears to be holding a cigar. Beside him sits another man who looks as if he might be an older brother or even his father. There are seven children and a nun. Everybody is immaculately turned out in Sunday best, and all are sporting flowers. What the occasion was, I have no idea.

At the 1969 Esperanto Congress, the Da met new friends from all over the world. In his book *Seo, Siúd agus Siúd Eile* (*This, That and the Other Thing*) he lists their names: Sylvie Bonnet from France, Ladislav Fiala and Olda Antos from Czechoslovakia, and Catherina Westerveld from the Netherlands. The week's events included lectures, films, concerts, and performances of different national dances. There were plenty of free drinks and cigarettes courtesy of sponsors such as Guinness, Powers and Carrolls. The Congress came to a close with an ecumenical service in the Trinity College Chapel. Finally, the delegates sang the Esperanto anthem 'La Espero'—and 'La Soldata Kanto', my father's translation of 'Amhrán na bhFiann', or 'The Soldier's Song'.

We were in Ballycastle when the Troubles exploded in August 1969. A postman pal of my father, Willie Crean, was supposed to drive us back to Belfast, but couldn't make it. There was rioting everywhere—cars were being hijacked and torched all over the city. We managed to get a bus to Belfast, where John McCavana picked us up at Smithfield Bus Station. We drove up the Falls, trails of smoke hanging over the streets, broken bricks, glass everywhere. Burnt-out buses, delivery vans, milk floats as makeshift barricades. At Dunville Park we had to turn left onto the Grosvenor Road. The Falls was blocked by a phalanx of RUC men.

The summer of the sixties was over. The electric crackle of conflict hung in the air, lurking in an uneasy silence, waiting for night to come stepping in again. My godmother Maureen Shephard had to move out of her house on the Kashmir Road.

In Springfield Park, our cousins the Browns made their escape. Barricades went up in the middle of the streets joining the Shankill and the Falls. Neighbour was cut off from neighbour along sectarian lines.

Then the soldiers came. They came to rescue the Catholics from being attacked, so we thought. They were welcomed with open arms, and many locals made them cups of tea. Their arrival was a thrill for the children, and I can remember soldiers taking me for a jeep ride around the neighbourhood. But it was only a matter of weeks before they were ransacking houses along the Falls, smashing religious statues, ripping up floorboards, wrecking furniture. In July 1970 a curfew was imposed on the Falls. Anybody could be shot after nightfall. No reason was needed. Five civilians were killed, sixty injured and 300 arrested. The Official IRA shot and wounded fifteen soldiers. In their invasion of the area, the Army used CS gas, and journalist Peter Taylor described how clouds of choking and suffocating gas suffused the streets, pouring out of alleyways. It got into people's eyes, noses, throats and lungs. Toddlers fell sick.

A war had begun in earnest. The Army took over. In a small state with a population of only 1.5 million people, some 27,000 soldiers were deployed in over a hundred bases.

On the Falls, people began to take sides—for or against the IRA; for or against the Provisionals or the Officials. Cumann Chluain Ard, against the odds, remained politically neutral, and for many years they had welcomed Protestants who wanted to learn the language. It was a policy they did their best to continue, but fear prevented the Protestants from coming.

My father had, during the 1940s, spent a brief spell in the

old IRA, before there were such things as Provies or Stickies. I only remember him talking about this once or twice. He told us he'd discovered his younger brother Pat was in the IRA, and begged him to let him join too. Pat tried to dissuade him, but the Da persisted, and finally became a volunteer. The Belfast IRA was poorly equipped at the time, not unlike the Dad's Army of the television comedy, a favourite show of my father's. It followed the antics of the pompous Captain Mainwaring's Home Guard platoon in the fictional town of Walmington-on-Sea; in the early episodes, the platoon drill with wooden guns and have no uniforms. So it was with my Da's experience in the IRA; he recalled training with broomsticks up on the Black Mountain.

He came to realise, though, that the time for using a real gun might come. The thought disturbed him. Could a true Christian kill his neighbour? The Da spoke to his confessor in Clonard Monastery, who advised him to listen to what his heart was telling him.

The Da left the IRA, but that didn't stop him from being interned in Crumlin Road Gaol. Apparently the police were on the hunt for Pat. Pat eluded them, and so they arrested the Da instead, whether by mistake or in spite I don't know. My father was only interned for a few weeks, but many years on he would still recall the indignity of being forced to walk naked in front of loyalist prisoners.

Shortly after the Da's funeral, we were told a story about his internment, and how he took on the State. On his release from prison, he returned to work, only to find that his pay had been docked for his time spent inside. He took a court case, logically arguing that since his employer and his gaoler were one and the same—the Royal Mail and His Majesty's Prison Service, in other words, the King—then it followed that his employer was the cause of his absence. Moreover, he had not been charged with any offence; it was clearly not his fault he had missed work. Not only did the Da get his pay, he set a legal precedent that benefited other servants of the State who had been interned without charge.

Andersonstown descended into fire and chaos. I remember our local record store, Caroline Records, in the aftermath of another session of rioting and looting. I walked into the still smouldering shell of the shop, pools of oily water, vinyl albums melted into furls, curls, plastic flowers. Another day I came home from school, and charred bank notes, lodgement slips, torn ledgers floated in the smoky air, the local Ulster Bank had been torched.

As the Troubles intensified, the sanctuary of Mooreland ended. Andersonstown became occupied territory. The British Army transformed our communal spaces into military camps. Casement Park was used as a helicopter base. Holy Child—my primary school—was a temporary billet. The military wards of Musgrave Park Hospital vanished behind a ring of steel and reinforced concrete. We still played football in the park, soldiers in observation towers watching us. Nothing was inviolate. I would step out my front door to find an Army patrol crouched in our garden. I would walk up Mooreland Park, aware that a gun was trained on my back. Snub-nosed Saracen troop-carriers—'pigs'—tore up the Andersonstown Road; teenage gangs rushed out from side streets to shower them with Molotov cocktails, paint-bombs, paving stones. At night I lay in bed listening to gun-battles raging for hours, the incessant back-and-forth chatter of SLRs and Kalashnikovs. On the anniversary of Internment Day, the eighth of August, the dawn would be greeted by the symphonic cacophony of binlid-bashing spreading through the city.

My brother Pat joined the Official Republican Movement but, like my father before him, found he didn't have an appetite for armed struggle. He was a Marxist at heart, and believed in class struggle and changing the consciousness of the masses. On his bookshelves titles by Jack Kerouac, Hermann Hesse and George Orwell rubbed shoulders with tracts by Karl Marx and James Connolly.

Pat was a political educator. New recruits would attend weekly talks on Pearse, Connolly, Guevara, the theory of revolution and so on. But he soon realised that his idealism was not shared by teenagers more intent on the adrenaline rush of being in 'the organisation'. He imagined them thinking, *Paddy, will you ever shut up and just give us the fucking guns?* He decided it was time to leave.

My father had little time for republicans who didn't support or understand Irish. During one election he refused to listen to a Sinn Féin canvasser who had addressed him in English. It is a mark of their well-oiled election machinery at the time that a second canvasser visited our house within the hour, apologising to my father in flawless Irish.

With the arrival of the Troubles, the linguistic lie of the land changed in my home. My mother spoke Irish less and less. Once it had meant freedom for her. She would still talk about how the best days of her life had been in Donegal, when the language meant clean air, little cottages, hillside walks, simple pleasures. But, in her mind, Irish was now linked to republicanism, to the IRA, to violence. She was afraid, I think, that if we were to be heard speaking Irish, we might be considered Provies. She would also remark that Irish wasn't much use when it came to getting a job.

Without knowing it, she was echoing an age-old theme. In 1936, Prime Minister James Craig had asked, 'What use is it, in this busy part of the empire, to teach our children the Irish language?' It was as if a centuries-old shame of the language had come back to visit us. It is not that long since the Catholic Church taught its flock that Irish was the 'language that confuses honest men'—something that seems hard to believe when we recall how the Christian Brothers relentlessly drilled us in Irish grammar. First the clerics ripped *an teanga*—the tongue—from our mouths, and then, generations later, and much too late, shoved it back down our throats.

By 1977, I was listening to the first punk records—fast, frenetic, three-chord garage-band music, ablaze with anarchic anger. Helicopters hovered over our house all night; the squawking walkie-talkies of Army foot patrols would sporadically echo down the street. After six, the city centre was a place of desolation and dread.

A night after a gig in 1979. We had no chance of escaping the National Front skinheads. Sweaty, our clothes soaked from two hours of pogoing to Stiff Little Fingers, we stood at the Falls Road bus stop—just outside Lord Hamill's Hamburgers. Still high from the music. Decky, Dee, Anio, Len and me. The skinhead gang—about a dozen of them—encircled us. They said nothing, they simply stared at us for a few brief seconds that seemed like an eternity, before rapidly moving in for the kill. One of them smashed a fist into my face and I fell back against the wall. I slumped to the ground, curling myself into a foetal position, and allowed the kicks to rain down on me. A police Land Rover passed by in the street and didn't stop. The skinheads finished their battering and ran off towards Great Victoria Street, back to Sandy Row.

We were lucky, really. We only got a bruising. We were alive; we escaped being stabbed or shot. Sheila Magee, Dee's mother, rang Queen Street RUC Station to ask why the police patrol didn't stop to help us. She was told there had been no patrol in the vicinity.

The Clash, Joy Division, The Buzzcocks and The Stranglers were the soundtrack of my teenage years, their brittle, edgy songs reflecting my violent urban reality. My Da was now in his sixties, seeking solace in the world of the Blasket and Donegal writers—Tomás Ó Criomhthain, Séamas Ó Grianna, and Mící Mac Gabhann. Wonderful stuff that I would only appreciate much later. Our cultures and worlds seemed oceans apart. I was thinking in English; he was dreaming in Irish. He saw the chasm growing between us. I was reading new-wave science fiction— revolutionary, surreal, dystopian, nihilistic fiction light years removed from my Da's beloved Jules Verne, H.G. Wells and Edgar Rice Burroughs. In my youthful arrogance, I saw my father dreaming of a mythical Gaelic land that could never be. He and his *gaeilgeoir* friends, I thought, lived in a room just off the reality I knew. I imagined them sitting in the corner of Cluain Ard in Hawthorne Street, recalling better days in Rann na Feirste, talking about the language itself hour after hour. Outside the city was on fire with hate. They were in their sanctuary.

At night I sat in the parlour, headphones on at full blast, listening to Hawkwind's space rock. They were the original psychedelic punks, and I lost myself in their hypnotic buzzsaw guitars, cascading synthesizers and spiralling saxophone riffs. Their sometime lead singer and conceptual auteur Robert Calvert took to the stage like some cosmic Biggles or Lawrence of Arabia, sporting World War II aviator gear and brandishing guns.

Calvert 'graduated from the same lunatic asylum' as his friend, science-fiction writer Michael Moorcock, editor of the controversial *New Worlds* magazine, which published early work by J.G. Ballard and D.M. Thomas. Calvert's song 'High Rise' took its inspiration from Ballard's novel of the same title, in which a utopian skyscraper community descends into barbarism. I loved to read Ballard's *Vermilion Sands*, retreating into its exotic vision of a surreal desert resort in the not-too-distant future—a world populated by cloud-sculptors, retired pilots and decadent movie queens; a sinister but seductive landscape of wind-yachts, poetry machines and singing plants.

My mother had her own way of escaping the darkness of Belfast. In the mid-seventies the Ma and I would go to the 'wee house', a gate lodge my Aunt Annie and Uncle Jackie were renting near Seaforde, not far from the estate of the last Unionist prime minister of Northern Ireland, Brian Faulkner. In this cottage we lived a fantasy of country life (there was no electricity): we cooked on a range, read by oil lamps. It was in the wee house that I once thought I saw a ghost. Annie, Jackie, cousin Martin, the Ma and myself sat by a wood fire on a late, drowsy, summer evening, playing cards. At the window I saw a dead man staring at me, his skin grey and yellow, his hands stretched towards me in supplication. I pointed to him—'Look, there's someone there'—but nobody else saw anything.

One of my Da's favourite books was *Fiche Bliain ag Fás* by Muiris Ó Súilleabháin. I have a copy now—a second edition from 1933, issued only months after the first edition, such was the demand. It describes a world apart, that of the Blasket Isles, or more specifically, An Blascaod Mór, the Great Blasket. Robin Flower suggested that the name might have derived from the Norse word *brasker*, a dangerous place.

Fiche Bliain ag Fás tells of a hard-working peasant community, of the rough-and-tumble of fishermen and their folk. It is also a world full of shadows and ghosts, apparitions. From the still depths of the sea there emerges a whale. On another occasion, some men in a *naomhóg* are visited by a ghost who warns them of an impending storm. In the chapter entitled 'An Torrámh' or 'The Wake', the author recalls being awakened at three in the morning, that time of the night sometimes described in Irish as *mí marbh na hóiche* or *marbhtrá na maidine*—the dead time of the night, or the dead beach of the morning. A neighbour comes with the news that Sean-Chait has died. The sea is *breá bog*, fine and gentle. There are voices and the boy Ó Súilleabháin listens. He falls asleep, and Sean-Chait, or rather, her ghost, is staring in the window at him. He screams, and his father, who tells him he's just imagining things, says, 'Look, it's just the cat.'

As Declan McCavana and I grow older, we remain in a gang of sorts. We start hanging out with Damien Magee, Martin and Brian Burns from Stockman's Avenue; Noel Burke from Gransha; Pete Hesketh and Paul Burke from Beechmount. Together, we go to punk gigs in the Ulster Hall, the Harp Bar, the Pound.

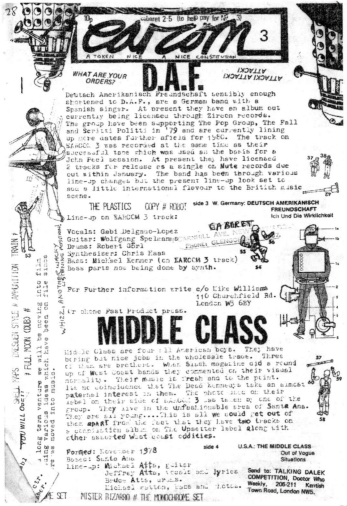

On Friday, 4 May 1979, I go to see the Mekons at the Harp, where I meet Ben Allen, the editor of local punk fanzine *Cabaret*. Ben's every utterance is bizarre, and I can never decide if he's chronically shy or just genuinely dislocated from reality.

He swims in the wilder shores of rock music and literature —Cabaret Voltaire, Captain Beefheart, William Burroughs. We live in the same city, but worlds apart—he comes from Newtownabbey, on the outer edges of North Belfast. We write to each other every week. My letters enthuse about Dexy's Midnight Runners and The Jam. Ben's communications are exercises in cultural obliteration. Newspapers, magazines, adverts, his friends' handwritten lyrics, photos, personal letters—these are all submitted to the scissors and rearranged into collages. One letter is designed to rip its contents when opened. He will frequently write on the inside of the envelope.

confused page ①

24.3.80

Ben Allen
1 Earnhill Avenue
Carnmoney

Dear BO
        I was talking about how weird Captain Beefheart was to Ken (drummer in allotropes who recently turned totally H.M. and is advertising his drumkit in the next NME £100) cabaret for sale £100) and he lent me a tape which he said his mate taped on the back of another taped for him. It wasn't Capt Beefheart it was L.A. Woman which I have played about 12-15 times. It has a real hatred of America in "L'America" which is alout it, but the rest of the songs I truly am verging on genius and the rest are just plain superb.
        It marks the beginning to me of a period of open mindedness for all music regardless of time, place, fads, crazes etc and also a disregard of at lot of conventional bands (gtr/drum/vcl's)   OPINION/CRITISISM

I got John Foxx no-one driving doublewigh readily explodes treason, Iggy Pop Too Mosquito and drums and wine XTC and Mr Partridge takes away the live of salvage LP's just to prove or disprove previous opinions and criticism

I have got £27 each from cabaret 3 and I should have £90

I still have a four-page letter from Ben. He can't spell, his handwriting is a cramped scrawl racing across the page. '*Cabaret* really fucks up and makes other magazines seem irrelivant.' 'If you understand why you bought an LP or understood a person's view on an LP you would throw it away.' 'People who wear anarchist t-shirts aren't anarchist because if you believed in anarchy, anarchy wouldn't exist to you.'

Declan—along with Pete, Damien, Noel and Paul— eventually forms the group Positive Action. A Positive Action Collective includes Seánie Doran and myself. The band's music reflects our listening—white reggae, the Gang of Four, Siouxsie and the Banshees, The Cure. Decky is the lead vocalist—he carefully avoids calling himself a singer, because he knows he hasn't got a note in his head. What he does have, though, is the ability to write lyrics, self-confidence and stage presence. In our friendships we evolve a collective ethos. For a long time, Declan, Brian Burns, Damien Magee and myself are an inseparable quartet. Here is a note I still have, a pact that outlines our principles:

1. No secrets or back-stabbing
2. Credit where due
3. No jealousy
4. Openness of opinion
5. Promotion of chances
6. No dictation of political, religious, personal attitudes
7. More humility
8. Continuation of democracy
9. Share and share alike
10. Total unity as far as possible

This ethos becomes the core of Positive Action. Declan promotes the idea of the 'Positive Revolt', where our enthusiasm, our hunger for learning, our belief in ourselves, will overcome Belfast's cynicism, apathy and violence. The band's logo is an arrow combined with a plus symbol. We put up stickers with this logo and the band's name everywhere—on buses, lamp-posts, phone kiosks. One day we're approached by a man who asks us, 'So is this a new political party or something?' Seánie and I become general gofers-cum-propagandists for PA, as we now call ourselves. This means we have to hoof amplifiers in and out of the Beechmount Leisure Centre, where Saturday after-noons are spent rehearsing and drinking coffee.

I contribute an article entitled 'positive action—a new approach' to Ben Allen's *Cabaret*. PA's songs are expressions of 'alienation, fear, hate'. The band's sound—'pete hesketh's unconventional drumming'; 'noel's essential bass lines'; 'dee's jagged guitar'—is a sonic echo of the songs' imagery of 'broken glass, concrete walls, nail bombs'. Decky goes to Dublin to see Roogalator and the Radiators from Space in Belfield. U2 in McGonagles. We visit Dublin together, and are mesmerised by the Dandelion Market, by the record shops, by the fact that the girls are more stylish. We all plan to go to Trinity College; Dublin is our destiny.

From the early seventies on, my parents become increasingly addicted to the news, tuning in to BBC Radio Ulster every hour to hear what is happening in the outside world, beyond the relatively safe environs of Mooreland. On particularly bad days, the horror mounts by the hour, the details emerging in depressing dribs and drabs. Somebody shot here, two more shot there in revenge. The death count from a bomb climbs as the day wears on. At first, the numbers are unknown. Then it is four, maybe more; by afternoon it is nine, by evening, twelve. Finally, the confirmed count the next day.

The Troubles are an endless terror for my mother. As soon as her sons or husband leave the house, she immediately begins praying for their safe return. In his final years in the post office, my father does the night shift in Tomb Street sorting office. He never feels safe walking to work through the deserted docklands. In Stockman's Lane, my brother Breandán is dragged into a Saracen armoured car by an Army snatch-squad. They rough him up before taking him to an RUC station, where he is charged with rioting. In court, two soldiers give wildly conflicting evidence. They don't even have the intelligence to lie convincingly. The judge dismisses the case.

It was also sometime in the early seventies that the Ma decided to convert the loft. Her children were older, bigger. An extra bedroom was called for. It was a basic conversion—the rafters were covered with boards, one tiny window looked towards Casement. In the winter it froze; in summer you stifled in its oppressive, airless heat.

My eldest brother Ciaran moved up to the loft, where he kept beautiful hardback notebooks on his desk. He practised calligraphy. He wrote poems about Saint Ciaran, monks, the insular Celts, and the new estates of Belfast. When he was out, I'd rifle through his poetry magazines. In one copy of *American Poetry Review*, I read an extract from Marjorie Perloff's *Frank O'Hara: Poet among Painters*; there was also a selection of O'Hara's poems, those bright remembrances of a life fully lived in the moment.

On his shelves were T.S. Eliot and William Blake; various books in the Fontana Modern Masters series, including Jonathan Miller's study of Marshall McLuhan; and *An Experiment with Time*—a bizarre book by J.W. Dunne about precognition and our experience of time. It was all the rage when it was first published in 1927, and obsessed J.B. Priestley and Eliot. Another book of Dunne's was *Nothing Dies*.

Dunne's theory—based on accounts of precognitive dreams —is that in reality all time is eternally present. In other words, the past, present and future co-exist. But the human brain experiences this simultaneity in linear form. Dunne suggests that, in dreams, this way of interpreting time ceases to be as concrete as when we are awake. A precognitive dream is consciousness freed to roam across past, present and future. Dunne posits that we exist on two levels, both inside and outside time.

One Christmas Ciaran gave me the science-fiction anthology *Tomorrow's Children*, which contained 'The Ugly Little Boy' by Isaac Asimov. It's the story of a Neanderthal boy who is snatched from the past by a time-travel research group, Stasis. His existence in the present threatens the very fabric of time and space, and so he is kept in a space he cannot leave. A nurse, Edith Fellows, is appointed his guardian. She learns this ape-like child is smarter than the scientists realise. Charmed, she names him Timmie. When they plan to return him to his own time, she fears for his life in a savage world he can longer comprehend. Edith decides she cannot abandon him, and together they vanish into the past.

My mother feared for us. Up in the loft, I would gaze out the window, across the darkness of Casement Park at night, trying to see what was going on outside, somewhere in the housing estates sweeping up the mountainside. Bursts of machine-gun fire, pistol shots. A helicopter would hover, its drone ebbing and flowing. 'Come away from that window, Liam,' my mother would plead from downstairs.

Nineteen seventy-nine is my last year at St Mary's, A-level time. Decky, Dee, Pete, Seánie, Noel and most of my mates are in the year below me. I never make it to Trinity—with the exception of English Literature, my results are awful. But I do become the only person in my year to attend University College Dublin. My first months in Dublin are insecure, lonely, as I try to find my feet. In Belfast, tensions are high as IRA prisoners in the H-blocks are preparing to go on hunger strike. In November 1980, Decky writes a long letter to me, urging me not to lose faith in myself. He also includes the lyrics of a few PA songs, including 'Today Is Different':

Wind blew and the sun rose high,
    high in the sky,
Clouds burst
        And the rain exploded
        Just like a nail bomb in Belfast.
Sun gives warmth,
The rain is cold,
Cold like beads,
Beads of sweat
            that the clouds discard
            that the clouds discard…

Oh I'm not normally touched by such things
But TODAY IS DIFFERENT…

Let's get back to the HATE of the city
Let's get back to the HATE of Belfast.

---

10. The flowers expand under the touch
        The life-giving touch of
    their father,
    Frequented by nature's finest
        —her chosen few.

Oh I'm not normally touched by such things
But   TODAY IS DIFFERENT,
They move me the wonder and the wonderous
                        touch
    of nature and her organs.
    lets get back to the HATE of the city.
    Lets get back to the HATE of Belfast."
    Bo I won't send you 'Turmoil' yet as I'm
    going to rewrite it but here's 'Ninth Heaven'

11. Coz I like it;
    "loud sounds crash, bang, make a din
    -Its the smash of another dust-bin.
    Shrill sounds singe, scream, scald, scorch,
    Nervous noises nestle 'neath another burning torch.

    Screaming sirens whisper hide themselves from view,
    Harassing horns hush - and overlook,
    Burning bonfires bustle with bloody brutish keys,
    Comprehension of their deeds is all but nil.

    These people can't believe no more
    In what
    theyre fighting for;
    A mindless conflict - useless - doubtless —
                        silly.
    But the loud sounds continue, year after year,
    controlled by a few, carried out by too many,
    Will they never understand
                        what we've written on the walls
    on Broadway and the Falls Road.
    We don't want 'Ninth Heaven' any more"

7

BA MHAITH
LIOM GABHÁIL
'NA BHAILE
I want to go home

In 1988 I return to Belfast after years in London. I move back into the loft.

In March of that year horror visits us. In Belfast the air is thick with fear, pregnant with danger and death. The Gibraltar Three are being buried. The three are Seán Savage, Daniel McCann and Mairéad Farrell—IRA volunteers gunned down by the SAS whilst planning a bomb attack in the tiny British colony of Gibraltar. The security forces were aware of their intentions, and sent in the SAS to deal with them. Their killings were the subject of much controversy. They were all unarmed, and none carried a remote control detonator at the time of the shooting. One witness quoted in Thames Television's investigation, *Death on the Rock*, said that the SAS team

> just went and shot these people. That's all. They didn't say anything, they didn't scream, they didn't shout, they didn't do

anything. These people were turning their heads back to see what was happening and when they saw these men had guns in their hands they put their hands up. It looked like the man was protecting the girl because he stood in front of her, but there was no chance. I mean they went to the floor immediately, they dropped.

I am working on a community scheme—Cathedral Community Enterprises—that is based in the old St Gall's Youth Club building in Milltown Cemetery. Because of the funeral, we're given the day off. I head into town to mosey around the bookshops. The Falls is off limits, so I return to Mooreland via the Lisburn Road, and I get off the bus at the King's Hall. As I walk up Stockman's Lane, I notice a puff of smoke coming from the direction of Milltown. A helicopter circles in the sky.

Later, back home, I find out what has happened. A rogue loyalist, Michael Stone, has attacked the mourners. The television footage is dramatic. Stone is crazed, a complete madman. He hurls grenades into the graveside crowds. There are frenzied shouts. 'He's got a gun!' Groups of young men chase him. There are the muffled cracks of pistol shots. People take cover behind gravestones. As Stone runs for the M1 motorway, he turns to fire and toss another grenade. Amongst his victims is Kevin Brady.

The morning of Kevin's funeral, I am in bed, hungover. I awake to the sound of sobbing: my father is in the kitchen, talking to the Ma, bursting into tears every now and again. I go down to find out what's wrong. 'It was terrible. Two men were killed. Loyalists attacked the funeral—this car came out of nowhere, then there were shots. And everybody went mad.' He is not sure what has happened, it has all been so fast.

I go up the street, to get *The Guardian*. At the top of Mooreland Park, there's an RUC man. I go over to him and ask him what's happened. 'I don't know. It looks like another loyalist attack.' He looks away from me, he has nothing more to say.

The full details emerge throughout the course of the day. The story is that two soldiers in plain clothes decide to drive up the Andersonstown Road, the reason is never made clear. They reach the funeral, and panic. They frantically reverse their car. They try to turn. Men surround the car, they clamber over it, hitting the windows with iron bars, sticks. One of the soldiers fires a shot. Eventually, they are dragged from the car, taken into Casement Park. My brother Breandán saw them dumped over a wall—like two carcasses in a butcher's shop, as he described it. They are stripped naked, then bundled into a black taxi, the driver cheering as he speeds off, waving a pistol. At the waste-ground behind the Mace supermarket they are shot dead.

This all took a matter of minutes. It was filmed from a helicopter. The next day, the papers carried a photo of Clonard priest Father Alec Reid kneeling over the bloodied body of one of the soldiers, administering the last rites. For days, the streets were filled with silence, doom.

When Breandán got home, his wife Pádraigín told him he looked grey. He swore they would move out of Belfast. His son Domhnall was only a few months old, and he didn't want him to ever see anything like the events of that day. A few years later, Breandán built his family's new house on a plot of land near

Loughinisland in County Down. It was a peaceful place, where Catholics and Protestants got on with each other.

But at 10:13 pm on 18 June 1994, whilst Ireland played Italy in the World Cup finals, two masked loyalists walked into the Heights Bar in Loughinisland, and riddled the place with machine-gun fire. Of the fifteen customers in the tiny bar, six Catholic men were shot dead. Aidan O'Toole, the son of the bar's owner, was one of the survivors. He refutes the UVF assertion that the bar was host to a republican function that night:

> There was never talk about religion or politics in the bar, no one was interested in that kind of thing. My father wouldn't have allowed it, no way. There are as many Protestants drink in the bar as Catholics. The killers set out to murder us all, Catholic and Protestant.

24 March 1998. I arrive just in time for my father's death. He has been in the Antrim Area Hospital for a couple of nights. Once we realise he's probably dying, I get the train to Belfast. Ciaran picks me up at Central Station. 'Well, he's still hanging on.' Caitlín, her husband Joe, Pat and Breandán are all there, sitting by his bed. My Da is wearing an oxygen mask, he has drips and electrodes attached all over. I go over and hug the Da, who smiles when he sees me. A doctor tells us that there can only be two visitors at a time, so Ciaran and I stay while the others head off for food. It looks like the Da has rallied round, as he has done so many times before. He has already survived numerous heart attacks. He might pull it off yet again. I tell him how I took part in the Saint Patrick's Day parade in Dublin, dancing down O'Connell

Street with a samba band; he is chuffed. The talking gets more difficult, though, for the Da. He rests for a while.

After a time, he is getting agitated—he seems uncomfortable no matter what way he lies. I nervously look at the heart-monitor screen. His arms jerk, lifting up together as if he is reaching for something. He starts talking. '*Oscail an doras.*' Open the door. The arms fall and rise again. I run to get a doctor, and she tells me that his heart is out of control, he needs to be given a shot, but it will involve a gamble, a risk. It might dangerously suppress his breathing. But there is little choice. Minutes later, he is going, rapidly, his heartbeat falling. Ciaran and I watch the heart monitor—'Look, his beat is up, he's okay.' But it's only the drugs keeping the heart going. The doctor and nurses administer CPR, they pummel his chest. They jolt him with a defibrillator. Nothing works, his body goes limp, lifeless.

A few years after his death, I read my father's diaries. They record the trivial details of his day-to-day life with the Ma, at home in Mooreland. What they have for tea, or dinner. Baked beans. Fish fingers. Meatballs. Bacon. Chips. What they watch on television. A Hercule Poirot film on Sunday, 5 January 1992. The news. On Friday, 17 January 1992, he notes the murder of seven workers in Tyrone.

He mentions the books he buys, hymn books and prayer books in Irish—*Gáirdín an Anama*. Or *Peadar Ó Dubhda: A Shaol agus a Shaothar*—a biography of a Dundalk language activist self-taught in Irish, and a former messenger boy like my father.

A new year's day entry mentions how—for the first time in his life—he has not gone to mass. It is too wet, too windy. He stays in the house all day, listening to Raidió na Gaeltachta. He goes to bed at half ten and fears that his start to the new year has been a bad one. On Saturday, 7 July 1990, a rainy day, he talks of his faith failing, and prays for help. He doesn't go to Cluain Ard, nor to mass. Throughout 1990, friends of his have heart attacks. Tom Heenan is terminally ill. Each diary entry has the saint day—*Féile na nAingeal Coimhdeachta*, the Feast of the Guardian Angels, on the 2nd of October. Tom dies that day. Cardinal Ó Fiaich—an acquaintance of my father's, and a lover of Irish—dies, and my father says, '*Ní bheidh a leithéid arís ann.*' His like will never be seen again. In Cluain Ard, there is sadness at the news. My father records nightmares in which he is hunted by an unknown presence, and falls out of bed. He attends the funeral of his close friend Alf Ó Murchú; the graveyard oration is given by singer and Cluain Ard stalwart Albert Fry. The Da declares: '*Tá mé mar a bheadh Oisín i ndiaidh na Fianna.*' I am like Oisín after the Fianna.

As the days go by, he worries about his health, he talks about how he wouldn't know what to do without the Ma around. His angina attacks are more frequent. He is losing sight in his left eye, which only sees a fog now. The Ma too is having a bad time of it, pains in her bones, blood pressure problems, nerves, anxiety. One morning she is depressed, she is finding it harder to cope with the household chores.

January and February 1992 are grim months. Early in the morning of Friday, 31 January, my nephew Séamas is killed in a car crash. My brother Pat drives my parents to Cushendun, where Séamas's remains are brought home from the hospital late in the evening. On the day of the funeral, Sunday, 2 February, my father returns home to the news that Paddy Clarke—one of his post office pals—has been shot dead by loyalists. That morning Paddy had set out for Séamas's funeral, but never made it as his car broke down. The next day a Protestant man is murdered in Dungannon. On Tuesday an RUC man walks into a Sinn Féin office and guns down three men before committing suicide. On Wednesday the UFF attack a betting shop on the Ormeau Road, killing five men. On Monday 10 February the Da writes that his mood is *dubhach agus duairc*, dark and joyless.

The Ma and Da age in what seems like a matter of months. I have finally left Mooreland, I'm living on South Parade. There is an account of my departure in his diary, dated Tuesday, 20 March 1990. He notes that he feels sad when I tell him I'm moving into a flat, but he knows that it's time for me to stand on my own two feet. He prays to Mary to wrap me in her cloak and to protect me from all harm.

My mother is hobbling more and more, until she can barely walk. The arthritis is wracking her body. Neither of them can handle the stairs anymore, and they have both moved into the parlour. There is a commode for the Ma to use. Sometimes she falls out of bed, and the Da is helpless, he cannot lift her. He rings Pat at three, four, in the morning. Pat will drive all the way across the city to help.

When I call to the house, most of the time now the Ma will nod off mid-sentence, she is sleeping more and more. The Da is prone to moods of despair; he is shaving less; he leaves the house less and less. He's afraid to leave the Ma on her own. Whole days, weeks are spent in the living room watching television.

Eventually the sanctuary of Mooreland itself is violated. In the early hours one morning, two gunmen smash open the kitchen door. They drag my father out of bed and use electrical cable to tie him to a chair. 'We're in the wrong house, for fuck's sake!' one of them shouts. But it makes no difference. His companion holds a gun to my Da's head and asks him where his money is. There is no argument, and my father tells him there's cash in the biscuit tin in the kitchen. A thousand pounds. They take the money, cut the phone line, warn the Ma and Da not to call for help for at least thirty minutes.

It was clear we couldn't leave our parents in Mooreland. My sister Caitlín took my father to her house near Cushendun. In his last few years, my father had a new life, a new home. Caitlín and Joe took him to the local pub, where he became a much-loved regular, and found a new audience for his songs and yarns.

But our mother needed around-the-clock professional care; she could no longer walk without help, was incontinent, and her memory was worse than ever. We took the terrible decision to place her in a nursing home, albeit not far from Caitlín's. The Ma comforted herself with the thought that this was a temporary measure, until she 'got better'. But as the days became weeks, and the weeks became months, anger and suspicion would sometimes possess her; she had been betrayed, and her worst nightmare was now a reality.

My mother was never the same. Taken from Mooreland, and from years of reassuring domestic ritual, she fell further into the oblivion of dementia. She began to speak Irish to me again when I visited. It became a secret language in which she would rail against the nursing staff, and how they couldn't understand that

94

there was nothing wrong with her. '*Ba mhaith liom gabháil 'na bhaile.*' I want to go home—this was her endless, heartbreaking refrain. Once outside the doors of the nursing home, I would burst into floods of tears. The thing my mother wanted more than anything else in the world was the one thing I couldn't give her.

After most of her children left home, my mother had changed the back bedroom into a shrine of sorts; the dressing table converted into an altar for her own mother. The grand-mother who died decades before I was born, whose name I don't even know. I only know her as a photo of a handsome-looking woman. My mother surrounded the photo with votive candles, flowers, and prayer cards. She would recite the rosary to herself here.

On my mantelpiece I have photos of my mother and father. One taken by a street photographer, it's their honeymoon. I recognise the place it was taken. Talbot Street, Dublin. There's the railway bridge behind them; you cross it on the DART these days. My Da is actually thin, he looks like I did when I was thirty. His hat is tilted to one side. He has a heavy overcoat. He's not wearing glasses. Was this before he needed glasses, or had he just taken them off? I don't know. My mother links arms with my Da, she's smiling. Her panda eyes remind me of my niece Róisín. The Ma's hair is tied up with a ribbon at the back. Between my parents a man looks directly at the camera; his coat, shirt and tie, and jumper are just like my father's.

A few weeks before my father dies, I have a sense there isn't much time left to ask the questions for which I need answers. 'Daddy, whatever was the story with Uncle Jack?' I ask on a visit to see him at Caitlín's. Jack is the Ma's brother. For all her life, she never spoke to me about him once. It was as if he never existed. I knew nothing about him. The Da pauses for what seems like ages, he stares out the window. He is uncomfortable with the question, and I am beginning to regret asking it. I realise he is crying. 'Your Mammy had a terrible time when she was a little girl. It was awful.'

Another black dream. My father returns from the dead. I'm sitting at home in Mooreland, telling the Ma that the Da has just died. But I turn and he is standing there. He takes his glasses off, wipes them, and puts them back on. I turn back to my mother to see her fall off her armchair, the newspaper slipping from her lap. I rush over to her, hold her in my arms. And like a vampire struck by sunlight in a 1930s horror movie, I see her age decades in seconds, her face wrinkling and collapsing. I panic, I tell her I love her. 'I know, Liam, you were always my wee boy.' These are her last words before she is a skeleton, and then dust.

8
CALL MOTHER A LONELY FIELD

In the nursing home, my mother loses her connection to memory. Her rituals of mass, pottering in the garden, tea with my father, familiar furniture, the knowledge of where everything is—these anchors to the present vanish. The past and the present melt into one another. She is in a place where her brain is fogged—parts of it work but don't link up to make sense of the images they are producing. So she tells Caitlín that she can see me. I'm there in the garden, 'Don't be silly, *there he is*,' hanging out the washing. I am as real to her as Caitlín and Pat and the rest of them in the room are. The actual Liam, the 38-year-old man living in Dublin, does not exist in her world, whilst the twelve-year-old boy who helps with the chores never dies. Inside the lulls in the snow-storm of her mind, hidden valleys of the past are glimpsed anew. Another time she is a little girl, not a hunched-up old woman in a nursing home. She is afraid to go to school. Why? 'Because the other girls all laugh and make fun of me.' Why's that? 'Because of Papa. Because he's always drunk.'

More frightening is a story my brother Pat told me only recently. He recalled visiting her in the nursing home. When he arrived, the Ma was in her bedroom, and there she was curled up in a ball on the bed, weeping like a little girl, repeating, 'Where am I? Where am I?' again and again.

December 1999, and my mother is dying. 'You won't recognise her, she's like a shrivelled-up little blackbird, her mouth is like a wee puckered-up cat's hole. Don't expect to see her looking like she did the last time you saw her,' Pat tells me when I arrive at the nursing home. My Mammy's arms are hooked like talons, her skin hanging loose. Her mouth is dry, furry. It looks sore. Her eyes are a million miles away, a swirling grey fog. Her breathing is a rasp. She can't speak. I don't know how much she sees, how much she hears, how much she knows. Does she know she's dying? We sit with her—Pat, Breandán, Caitlín, her daughter Róisín, myself. She drifts in and out of sleep. Breandán is talking to her, loud. 'Are ye alright there, Mammy? Do you want to go to sleep?' She awakes with a jolt. Caitlín says, 'God, he's a big eejit, isn't he, always roaring?' My mother bursts out laughing. It is the last laugh she'll have.

It is three or so in the morning, and I am walking down the loanen from Caitlín's house, heading for the nursing home. I plan to take over the sitting from Caitlín. It is pitch black, and I carry a torch to light my way. The wind whips my face. It is howling, keening, moaning. Trees shake, creak, leaves are a host of rustling. I can only make out the immediate road ahead of me. I float through the darkness of the fields, through the primal, fearful midwinter dark. My mother is dying as the light fades from the world, as it hurtles towards the shortest day. I lean into the wind, not awake, not asleep.

Caitlín has been up for hours, but decides to stay with me. We sit by my mother, watching every rise and fall of her fragile body. It is strange, this watching death being enacted in life. Each breath, each sigh. Each twitch of her shoulder. Each blink. 'Look, her hand moved.' Her breathing stops and starts. We are on a helter-skelter ride that never seems to end. The Ma's mouth is utterly parched; a nurse comes in now and again to give her a little water. I look at the nurse's records—it is nearly a week now since my mother ate anything remotely solid. Ice cream once in a while. Her eyes seem to open, but we don't know if she's still there in any conscious sense. The nurse speaks to her as I hold my Ma's hand. 'Mary, Mary, are you still in there? Can you hear us? If you're there, give us a wee sign. There's your Liam there, give his hand a squeeze to say hello.' She squeezes my hand. This is the last touch at the threshold of here today and gone tomorrow.

Hours later, Ciaran comes to take over. Caitlín and I go back to the house to sleep. I don't know if I actually do sleep or not. I drift through dreamscapes, I hear voices, and then the voice is real. It's Ciaran; he's rushed back up to tell us the moment is here. 'She's going.' We go back to the home, and my mother's room is crowded with nursing staff. A crucifix. A burning candle. Her eyes shut, her breathing imperceptibly shallow, minuscule little inhalations. Her skin appears to pulse with waves of colour, blood trying to pump up to her cheeks, waves of pink, purple, yellow and white. Light is seeping through her skin. She finally lets go, she folds. The breathing sinking more and more, each fall and rise slighter and slighter. Then it stops. 'She's gone.' It is only a short time—seconds—and the prayer begins, and we join in. 'Hail Mary full of grace, the Lord is with thee…'

The afternoon of the day we bury the Ma. I've just left the Gravediggers, had enough drink, not up for more talk, my eyes swollen and heavy. I've hardly slept for a week. I collapse onto the camp bed in the parlour. This was my space for years, where I did my homework, where I had coffee and fags with Noel Burke, listened to Captain Beefheart; where I did *The Guardian* crossword when I was on the dole; where I sat with friends sharing teenage angst. This was where the stereo was. I have a letter from my mother—'The house is quite lonely now without the stereo going but I suppose you will make up for that when you come home…' I fall asleep.

I awake to an aching loneliness. Here I am in Mooreland on my own, with nobody to talk to. There aren't even any ghosts, the ghosts left a long time ago. The walls have shrunk; the dimensions of everything—the walls, the stairs, the hallway— have shrivelled into smallness. This void is not home. I leave for the Dublin train.

Another letter from my mother, in 1987.

I went up to the loft today to tidy it up a bit, there were lots of books lying on the floor. I don't know if you left them there, I feel rather sad when I go up to it the years seem to have flown past but I suppose that is life here today and gone tomorrow.

Now she is gone, my father is gone. My childhood is gone.

I collect all the letters from my parents that I still have, and put them in chronological order, using my various addresses as a rough guide. Dublin—Balally Drive, Raglan Road, Mountjoy Square, South Circular Road; London—Brixton, Stockwell, Elephant and Castle, Peckham, Kennington; Israel—the Negev Desert, the Golan Heights. The message is always the same— *We were glad to get your letter, and to hear you were well; we were worried that you were sick or had moved again.*

Here I am on the long journey from Belfast to London. The train to Larne, the boat to Stranraer. The ferry's bar full of drunken loyalists, the slow haul through Scotland and England, the train crawling down the densely built-up backbone of urban Britain. Stuck in Crewe in the wee small hours. Arriving in the morning rush hour in a cold, cold London. Brixton under snow, huddling around a battered electric heater to keep warm. Here I am in Israel, it's 1986.

> Do you hear anything about all what is going on about the bombing of Libya? I am really worried about your safety or if you would be stranded there, because of Britain being involved in this bombing. They have killed British and American citizens even a fellow teaching in a University in Beirut has been kidnapped, being Irish does not make any difference his people have sought the help of the Irish embassy to get him freed—just let us know Liam what is happening in your vicinity you seem to be so far away it seems like another world to me.

I get glimpses of what is happening back home, full of an unintentional black humour:

> There is nothing unusual happening here except last night they burned two buses on the road because of Gerry Adams and

three others who were with him in a car were shot maybe you have heard about this.

Throughout the winter of 1986, she describes loyalist protests against the Anglo-Irish Agreement. On 17 October, she tells me she is writing by candlelight; the electricity has been off since tea-time, and there is only a supply for five or six hours a day. The nights are getting darker. She mentions that my cousin Ann Mooney is dying of cancer, she is praying for her. On 14 October, she wonders if I have a television, and if I have seen the news that 'tomorrow the town will be taken over by the loyalists, so God knows what will happen after that'.

writing in this kind of light We have been using these candles all week and they are getting smaller and everyone is buying them so we are hoping that it may be settled soon at least the weather has been great which gives us a boost.

One band I listened to in the parlour in Mooreland was Doll By Doll. They appeared in the early 1980s, the aftermath of punk. Their dramatic fusion of heavy rock, psychedelia and pop threw listeners, as did their lyrical use of work by e.e. cummings,

Kenneth Patchen, Anna Akhmatova, Louis MacNeice and others. Nobody quite got where they were coming from, and after a few years they vanished into oblivion. Some ten years later, after rescuing himself from failure, heroin addiction and destitution, their lead singer, Jackie Leven, released 'Call Mother a Lonely Field'.

And now the places that I love allow me no returning
The shining dreams of winter skies
The sadness and the burning
The ferries vanish in the snow
We telephone our children
I'll never love like this again
I couldn't lift the burden
And like young Irishmen in English bars
The song of home betrays us
Call Mother a Lonely Field

Jackie Leven tells me where the inspiration for this song came from. He was walking one very cold winter morning by the river Thames, near Maidenhead, with the sun blazing down.

Something about the way the frozen ground lay by the wooden fence at the water's edge, with mist coming over the riverbank, made me very lonely for my mother, reminded me of her loneliness when I was a child and how I worried that it was all my fault and that I could never be big enough to help her, or myself, through this distress. The furrows were hard with frost. And I had—suddenly—this tremendous urge to see my Mum. To me, her personality and who she was, was this kind of very beautiful and very frosted thing.

Mo Mháthair Sa Teach Banaltrais

'ba mhaith liom gabháil 'na bhaile'
'sé dúirt sí liom
cumhaigh sa cheol a chan sí
arís agus arís
go dtí go deo
'ba mhaith liom gabháil 'na bhaile'
'sé dúirt sí liom
caoineadh sa cheol a chan sí
arís agus arís
go dtí go deo
'ba mhaith liom gabháil 'na bhaile'
'sé dúirt sí liom
gol sa cheol a chan sí
cosúil le leanbh ar lorg a mháthar
a cuid súile lachtacha liath
ag iarraidh orm arís agus arís
go dtí go deo
í a thabhairt 'na bhaile
fiú amhain
nuair a fuair sí bás
níor thug muid
'na bhaile í

9
TEARMANN
sanctuary

My father now pops up in the books I read. In Máirín Nic Eoin's *Trén bhFearann Breac*, he is referred to in a chapter about Seán Ó Riordáin, and their ideas of linguistic sanctuary are compared. In *Our Own Language* by Gabrielle Maguire—a study of the Shaw's Road *Gaeltacht* in Andersonstown—a young reader is quoted saying that Liam Mac Carráin is the only writer he likes in Irish, because he's writing about the city, Belfast, and he's funny. He's not writing about farms and fish. In Brian Ó Maoileain's *An Cheallúnach*, a character wonders if he'll ever have Irish as good as that of Liam Mac Carráin. In my father's own diaries there are fond mentions of Brian. In 2009, Joe Mitchell—one of the leading lights in the Shaw's Road community—dies. At his wake, his son Domhnall, and a good friend of mine, gives me a little notebook.

Méid (1ú f.)
leis an méid
sa mhéid
leath an méid

Méid (2ú b)
Cén mhéid atá
ionat anois
Tá siad ar aonmhéid

Cuir in ord iad de
réir méide

Bhí méid mhór daoine
ann — dul i méad
Dá mhéad airgead (iaghad)
Cá mhéad airgid?

Bhí na hoilithirigh chráifeacha
le léir fá réir aréir agus iad
ag gabháil ar oilithreacht go
Teampall Pheadair sa Róimh.
Bhí an tEaspag Ó Domhnaill
agus an tAthair Ó Súilleabháin
na bhfochair ag an ché i
nDún na nGall ag fanacht le
teacht na loinge a bhéarfadh
iad thar muir chun na
Cathrach Síoraí agus bhí an
uile dhuine ag guí go
bhfuígheadh siad faill
labhairt leis an Phápa agus
le linn an turais chuir siad a
lán paidreacha suas ar an
intinn údaí

In my Da's handwriting, there are dozens of notes for explaining Irish grammar, mostly using nonsense yarns to lay bare the genitive case. My mother appears to me in my own voice, as I talk to my daughter Eithne. 'You skittery wee ghost,' I say, a phrase she would use with toddlers. I've often wondered where the word skittery comes from. I have somewhat fancifully imagined it is from the Irish *scoithim*, defined in Dinneen as 'I cut, pass, leave behind, drop, shed, excel, surpass'. *Scoitheas é*. I passed or outran him. My brother Ciaran, however, thinks it simply derives from 'the skitters', or diarrhoea.

One day the Da told me he needed to have an important discussion. He knew it wasn't always easy for me to speak in Irish, and that I was living in a new world very different to that of his youth. If I wanted to use English, he would understand. '*Maith go leor*,' I said, that's fine. We continued to speak in Irish.

I was afraid to break his heart, to fail him, or to betray what he loved most.

At college in Dublin, and then in the squats of 1980s south London, I spoke Irish very rarely. Occasionally it would emerge as a drunken party piece. At times I would cringe listening to myself, speaking to people who hadn't a clue what I was saying.

At Christmas, I would come home. My father's greeting was always the same—first a bear hug, and then the questions, 'An bhfuil ocras ort? Ar mhaith leat friochú?' Are you hungry? Do you fancy a fry-up? On one of these visits, he told me that he had no idea what I did with my life, but that he wanted me to know that there was always a home for me to return to, where himself and my mother would respect my privacy. There would always be food and a bed for me. A haven I could come to if I was in trouble.

I remember my first visit to the *Gaeltacht*—to Mín a' Chladaigh—at the age of eleven. Shy and alone, I wanted to go back to Belfast. *Cumhaidh* is what gripped me—pining, loneliness, homesickness, a soreness of the heart, longing. This Irish word contains in its sound an ache that no English word can evoke for me. Like *tocht*—an oppression, a catch in the throat or at the heart, a fit of grief, silence in the face of overwhelming emotion—it is a word my father often used when looking back at the lost world of his youth.

Decades later, 2003, my girlfriend Niamh and I are in Donegal, where she is touring her children's puppet show, *Luichín na Cathrach agus Luichín na Tuaithe*. I make an effort to speak Irish to the venue organisers, and begin to feel comforted by its sounds and its rhythms. Part of me feels that I am at home here. On our way towards Gaoth Dobhair we discover a townland called Tearmann.

In his book, *Na Glúnta Rosannacha* (*The Generations of the Rosses*), Niall Ó Donaill tells the history of the remote Rosses area between Gaoth Dobhair and Gaoth Beara. Before the Great Hunger, there was nothing one could actually call a road, it was a place apart. Ó Donaill's account of his people's history is a book of invasions. He tells of a people driven to eke out an existence by rocky shores or on mountainous extremes. The history of Donegal is one of occupation, usurpation, theft, betrayals, shoddy deals, seizures of land, the routing of whole populations. The one thing that protects the people of the Rosses from these seemingly endless assaults is a brave attempt to maintain their continuity of identity within language.

At the heart of the Rosses' mythology is the tale of Conall Caol and of his church, also known as *tearmann*. Legend has it that Conall carried *an leitir Íosa*—the letter of Jesus—from Rome to Ireland. It was believed that this sacred message or epistle had descended to earth from heaven in a forgotten city in the distant east, and was written by Jesus Himself. The letter urged *na fíréin*—the righteous men—to guard Sunday as a day of rest. Conall travelled afar to procure the letter. He eventually arrived at the church in which it was housed in Rome. There, on the steps of the altar of the Apostle Peter, he ordered the priest who was the custodian of the letter to remove it from its seal so that it could be copied. The priest fainted with shock. Whilst he struggled to recover, Conall quickly copied the letter.

Conall Caol's *tearmann* protected holy writ, words penned by the hand of God. In *Na Glúnta Rosannacha*, the Irish language is a lightning conductor from the other world to this world. Language links the generations. For centuries there was no such thing as reading or writing. The people's mind, spirit, disposition —*a n-intinn*—survived through song and storytelling.

Each generation recast the old stories—of exploits and feats —that had been handed down from father to son, from mother to daughter. They were shaped afresh as it suited them, fitting them into the mould of the people and places they were familiar with. Thus were the past and the present fused, reconciled.

In our bed and breakfast at Dún Lúiche, the *bean an tí* asks if I have a *cúpla focal*—a few words. '*Giota beag níos mó ná sin*,' I reply—a wee bit more than that. From then on, she mostly speaks Irish to me. There is a willingness to connect, and to make me feel at ease with what is undoubtedly my inferior Irish.

We travel to Gleann Cholm Cille, where we pay a visit to the Oideas Gael bookshop. There I buy a couple of poetry collections by Cathal Ó Searcaigh—and *Sruth Teangacha/Stream of Tongues*, by Gearóid Mac Lochlainn. This book shatters my ignorant notions of what exists within Irish literature. I realise what I have missed by not reading Irish. It is not the purely nostalgic literature I once imagined; it can be very much of the present. Mac Lochlainn writes about my home—west Belfast— and learnt much of his Irish from my Da. I recognise myself and my city in these poems. Here are the binlids, the soldiers, the helicopters, the sirens, the half-bricks, the plastic bullets and the Molotov cocktails. Here are people listening to Linton Kwesi Johnson and smoking spliffs. Here are people swimming between Irish and English. I learn that some of the most engaged, innovative, and beautiful writing emerging from Ireland is in

Irish. I am like a thirsty man, drinking from a long-forgotten well. *'Caithfear pilleadh arís ar na foinsí,'* says Ó Searcaigh—we will have to return to the springs. Soon I am also reading Mac Grianna's *Mo Bhealach Féin*; Padraic Ó Conaire's *Deoraíocht*; and eventually Ó Criomhthain's *An t-Oileánach*—all books full of utter strangeness, doorways into other worlds. Within these books I am simultaneously at home and dislocated.

My father has been dead eleven years now. I am now older than he was when I was born. In photographs I see the contours of my face beginning to resemble his. What survives most of him is his voice, and the Irish language. When I dream of him, he is always speaking in Irish. I am beginning to dream more often in Irish.

Sometime in the 1980s, I heard my Da use the word 'fuck' for the first—and only—time in my life. If we'd said that word as children he'd probably have washed our mouths out with soap. He was telling me how upset he'd been by a recent trip to the Donegal *Gaeltacht*. He was with some pals, and I imagine Father Des Wilson may have been their driver. They got lost looking for a friend's house, and stopped to ask directions. My Da approached a house, where he knocked on the door. As the *fear an tí* came out, the Da heard him talking to his wife in Irish. Naturally the Da addressed him in Irish, but got an answer in impolite English. My father was mortified, and switched to English himself. 'Seeing your English is so good, you'll know what I mean when I say fuck off.'

He wrote of how he saw the *Gaeltacht* of his youth vanish. Irish was slowly dying in the west. The television sets had taken the place of the storytelling, the people were silent before the flickering screens, nobody went out visiting any more. He went on to see hope in the cities, and in this, I hear echoes of Máirtín Ó Cadhain, who admired Belfast Irish speakers for their spirit and seriousness of intent.

There is the famous story of Humboldt's Parrot. Legend has it that in 1804, Prussian naturalist Alexander von Humboldt was exploring the Orinoco when he encountered an Indian tribe. When he asked them why their parrots spoke a different language from theirs, he was told that the parrots had belonged to the extinct Atures tribe. Humboldt's own account tells us:

> It is to be supposed that the last family of Atures did not die out until a long time afterwards: since at Maypures—bizarrely— there still survives an old parrot that nobody, say the natives, can understand, because it speaks only the language of the Atures.

The story comes in different versions. In one, Humboldt and his companion come across a cave in which lie the dead bodies of the Atures, who have been massacred by another tribe. By the cave lives an old parrot, the only survivor of the slaughter, the last speaker of Maypure.

On a website I discover that there is a project in which artist Rachel Berwick has taught parrots this dead language. Two young birds are chosen to ensure that they have not been polluted by English. 'Only Maypure spoken beyond this point' reads a sign in the laboratory.

For Berwick—who exhibited the birds in a hand-painted aviary—the parrots 'could be the sole and imperfect conduit in which an entire tribe's existence could be traced'. Her living linguistic installation was designed to 'reflect on the imperfection of memory, the permanence of loss, and our desire to recover that which is gone'.

Writer Padraic Ó Conaire surely had Humboldt's Parrot in mind when he wrote his story 'Aba-Cána-Lú'. In an old Chinese history book, the narrator tells us he has come across the story of the ancient civilisation of the *Aibitíneach* people, who lived in a land whose rivers teemed with fish, where there was rice, tea and coffee aplenty. They were despised by their neighbours, *muintir an Phártaigh*, and their mortal enemies destroyed their cities and temples. Almost every man and boy-child was slaughtered. Worse was to come. The gods themselves turned their backs: '*chuir na déithe cosc le drúcht na h-óiche*', the gods put an end to night-time dew. Every well dried. Disease crippled the population. Echoes of Cromwell's massacres and the Famine. The tale ends with the last survivor of the *Aibitínigh* waking from an exhausted sleep to the maddening cackle of crows. He wanders through a desert in search of food and drink. He finally comes to a cairn of bones. It is then he hears a voice calling in his own language, 'Aba-Cána-Lú!' He imagines it is his son speaking to him, but he is too weak to respond. As he takes his last breath, he looks up to see a parrot repeating 'Aba-Cána-Lú'. The history book tells us, 'We would never know such a people or such a beautiful country existed, if it was not for the account in our book.'

I know my own Irish is emaciated. But this is true for any Irish speaker, to a greater or lesser extent. In Gleann Cholm Cille in Donegal, my sister Caitlín introduces me to Liam Ó Cuinneagáin of Oideas Gael, a local man fighting to preserve

Irish in the district. He stretches his arms wide and says this is how much Irish my grandfather had; he narrows the gap to the width of his body, and this is how much my father had; finally his hands pull closer again, and this is how much I have.

Poet Liam Ó Muirthile talks about how Seán Ó Riordáin spoke of an *teanga seo leath-liom*—this language half-mine—as a type of stigma.

> I think of it in the opposite fashion. I've always known *an teanga* was *leath-liom*. I'm constantly going from *leath* to *leath*. And *leath* plus *leath* equals one. That means wholeness. In a sense, our duty is to forget the language and to learn. We don't have any sounding-box left, there are no values left. Who's to say my Irish is better than yours, or yours better than mine? It's ridiculous, I speak whatever I speak.

Gearóid Mac Lochlainn sees fear as the impediment to speaking Irish.

> That's where a lot of the hang-ups still are… a fear of sounding incompetent—or not fluent. As if we could all be naturally totally fluent in Irish, which is hypocrisy. I'm learning words every day. It's a constant process. Even fluency in English is a continuum. Personally, I began learning Irish at the age of eleven and still count myself proudly as a learner, a perpetual one. I learned most of my Irish in Belfast from the older people—that included Liam Mac Carráin, the storyteller, and lots of great *sean nós* singers that were very traditional.

Mac Lochlainn is also

> interested in Lee Perry, the way he would mix stuff, with samples, echoes, reverb. It was all picked up later in hip-hop, scratching,

taking anything from any song, James Brown, guitar riffs, and working out lyrics on top of it. It's the whole exploration of oral culture, how rebellion passes itself on in an oral way. And that's linked in with how I learnt Irish, it was a part of life, *ó bhéal go béal*, from mouth to mouth.

'*Ba mhaith leat gabháil áit eigin suimiúil*,' my daughter Eithne says to me—you want to go somewhere interesting. What she really means is '*ba mhaith liom*', or I want. It literally means 'it would be good with me'. Her Irish is *droim ar ais*, a little back-to-front, where *tú* and *mé*, you and me are all mixed up. She doesn't have this problem in English:'I love you,' she says to her mother.

'*Cén focal atá ar ghluaisteán?*' she asks; what she actually means is what is the word for a car in English. She is two-and-a-half years old, and she is learning that there can be many words for the one thing. English sentences come out, as if they have been bubbling underneath the surface of her Irish all along. She knows the past and future tenses now, and the future tense is power and promise. '*Rachaimid chuig áit éigin eile*'; we'll go somewhere else. What she does not know the word for is defined as *rud éigin*—something, a vague thing. I trawl through dictionaries to see if the thing she is talking about actually has a word in Irish. In the supermarket, she asks me what to call '*an rud sin*' (that thing), pointing to the conveyor belt at the cash desk. For a minute, Niamh and I struggle to remember what it is in English, never mind Irish. It's a thing that conveys things. A conveyor belt. What's the Irish?'*Crios taistil*,' I speculate, a travelling belt. '*Cad é sin?*' asks Eithne again. '*Crios taistil*,' I tell her. Later I look it up on the web, and find the official version is *crios iompar*, a carrying belt.

At night she swims in her river-talk of sleep-time babble,

infant ululations, warbles and cooing, snatches of songs. She translates as she talks: *sráid*, street; *i lár na sráide*, in the middle of the street; *suas síos*, up and down.

At bedtime I sing to her. '*Níl sé 'na oíche ná ina mhaidin.*' It's neither day nor night, it is not quite dark, it is not quite bright, it is the inbetween time. Other times I repeat a line from Michael Davitt, '*Titeann an oíche gleann ar ghleann.*' The night falls, glen by glen.

I pay a visit to 3 Mooreland Drive, where my nephew Fionntán now lives. Not much of the Carson presence remains. I open the door to my sanctuary under the stairs, and reach to the shelf just inside. I find the last vestiges of my model howitzer, part of the chassis, a wheel. I take them out for a brief look, and then put them back.

I have one of my occasional night terrors. It is dark and I am trapped in a haunted house. I have four or five companions. We are frightened, speaking of the shadowy flickers and sinister whispers we have all seen and heard. The house is old, going under a sea of darkness. Its floors are bare. The wallpaper stained and tattered. I come across some small furry rodents; they're cuddly, like little brown hamsters. I pick one up, and as I lift it toward my face to study it, it grows talons. Its soft hairs become sharp porcupine quills. Its pink mouth and nose merge to become a beak, which it opens wide. From this gaping yellow beak comes a translucent slug-like creature that slides into my open, astonished mouth. In the midst of its glowing sludge, I see a countless series of fizzling holograms, and I know each one is a memory, a moment in time. Each fleeting moment of my life is being sucked out of me, dredged from the realms of dream. As they issue forth, faster and ever faster, I shake with terror, watching myself become an empty vessel before my very eyes. I awake screaming, struggling not to fall back into this dream, forcing myself out of bed, onto my feet.

Mooreland has changed and I am not in its present. It is harder to see its past. People live and die. Houses live and die. Or they are renovated and shape-shift into something new. I try to remember Mooreland's changes over the years. One year I kept frogspawn in the old sink at the bottom of the garden. The house was an ongoing project for my mother; the very process of its maintenance sustained her. A fresh paint job outside every few years; the kitchen refitted; a coal fire replaced with an electric one.

In 1972, nearly 500 people are killed. On 21 July, the Provisional IRA kill nine people in the Bloody Friday bombings. I watch the news, horrified by images of firemen shovelling charred body parts—arms, legs—into plastic bags. Meanwhile, Bobby Fischer is crushing Boris Spassky at the World Chess Championship in Reykjavik. Chess has become a craze. In the midsummer heat, I play chess with Ciaran, sitting on the front doorstep. I devour chess books and magazines. I try to think what it might be like to be Fischer, who remembered every move, every variation.

I remember the kids wildly shrieking, screaming and giggling at dusk, the sun slipping below the Black Mountain. Our folks and their like are going or gone—into death or dementia. Their time for living and for generation is gone. Near Mooreland, fields disappear as new apartments and industrial estates mushroom. The Casement Park of my childhood—complete with swamps, ashy slopes, trees, tangled briars, miniature jungles—is mostly gone now, the old grass banks buried beneath concrete terracing. Its dark places are now obliterated by the glare of floodlights.

In his final days in the Glens, my father rarely went back to Belfast. The city that lived in his mind was long gone, he ached for things swallowed in the maw of time, the mills, the trams, and old train stations. In his book *Seo, Siúd agus Siúd Eile*, he wrote of his last visit to *an pháirc bheag* (the little park) or Dunville Park. He describes walking around the dried-up fountain. McBrearty's old sandstone house is gone; there are no longer any 'summer houses' or sandboxes. In his mind he hears the song 'The Old House':

> *Why stand I here like a ghost and a shadow?*
> *'Tis time I was moving; 'tis time I passed on*

On the day my father's friend Joe Mitchell is buried, I pay a visit to Harry Hall's bookshop on Gresham Street before getting the Dublin train. There I come across books my father once had—lots of poetry by Robert Service; and *The Imitation of Christ* by the mystic Thomas à Kempis. It is a book the Da treasured. In Chapter 23, à Kempis meditates on death:

> *This day a man is and tomorrow he appeareth not...*
>
> *When it is morning think thou shalt not come to the even...*
>
> *For thou has here none abiding city...*

About four months later, I decide to return to Harry Hall's, only to see a 'for sale' sign on a shuttered shop. The next day I meet up with Declan McCavana, back from Paris to visit his mother in a nursing home. We discuss the past, and I learn for the first time that Seánie Doherty, our childhood Pied Piper, died a number of years ago.

On the same visit I go to the Ulster Folk and Transport Museum, where I am delighted to find a tram my father journeyed on in 1954. It is number 357, a 'Chamberlain' tram, one of fifty ordered by Belfast Corporation in 1930. It was a state-of-the-art machine in its time, fitted with spring seats covered in brown leather, and even furnished with electric heaters. After the city tram system shut down on 27 February 1954, it was tram 357 that my father boarded for the last journey from Ardoyne Depot to Mountpottinger Depot.

My father did make one further tram journey, though. It was Saint Patrick's Day and he had the day off. I must have been six or so at the time. Breandán reminded the Da of a long-standing promise to take us to the Transport Museum, then in Witham Street. '*Rachaimid*,' said the Da, we'll go. When we reached the museum, my father had no interest in the trains, fire engines and cars. His heart gladdened when he saw the trams. Up we went on an old tram that was open. The Da sat down and shut his eyes, and for a little while his childhood flooded back. He was no longer a father with his two sons but a wee boy with his daddy, travelling to Greencastle. When he opened his eyes again, they were moist with tears. From that day on, he never dreamed of trams again.

Will Irish survive? Nobody knows. If it does, it will not be the language of the past, because we are not the people of the past. But a generation ago, men and women like my father and mother gave their children something that still fights erasure. If it endures it will be because there must always be a return to one's own *tearmann*, where something of one's soul and being is kept alive. It is a blessing that—finally—I have returned to the linguistic sanctuary my parents bequeathed me, for which I am eternally grateful.

Scríobh go luath le do thoil – fiú amháin cupla líne.

Bhí mé i Rann na Feirste ar feadh cupla lá le linn Seachtain na Cásca agus bhí am fíormhaith agam. Bhí féile mhór ar siúl sa Choláiste agus bhí ceol, craic, scéalaíocht, céilithe agus a lán rudaí eile ag gabháil ar aghaidh. Bhain mé aoibhneas as a bheith ag caint le seanchairde agus bhí an aimsir galánta. Thiomáin muid thart fá bhun an Eargail agus fán Mhucais agus thug muid cuairt ar theach Albert Fry ar Oileán Cruite. Bhí achan duine ag cur do thuairisce.

Tóg do pheann agus scríobh anois!

Grá 7 beannacht Dé
ó Dheaidí

My Father's Dreams

Is iontach an rud é
After all these years
Ach tá tú ann go fóill

I do bhrionglóidí
You'd find me
Caillte sa dorchadas

Gaineamh beo ag bogadh
Forever drowning
In aice leat

Doiligh mé a shroicheadh
Just a fingertip away
Ró-fhada uait

Le fada an lá anois
You've been gone
Tríd an doras

Idir beatha is bás
Now your hand reaches
Ó dhomhain do-mharfa

Tú ag caint liom
From far away
'Tabhair dom do lámh'

As anáil, le grá
You whisper in Irish
Do bharróg ag breith orm

ACKNOWLEDGMENTS

I would like to thank Jackie Leven for kindly allowing me to use the title and lyrics of 'Call Mother a Lonely Field'; the song can be heard on his excellent album *The Mystery of Love is Greater than the Mystery of Death*, available from Cooking Vinyl.

Thanks to Declan McCavana for the lyrics of 'Today is Different', and to Ben Allen for permission to use material from *Cabaret* fanzine and personal letters.

A special thanks to Barry Windsor-Smith and Alex Bialy of the Windsor-Smith Studio (www.barrywindsor-smith.com) for the exquisite drawing of Conan on page 58.

I would also like to thank Ciarán Ó Pronntaigh and *An tUltach* for permission to use the images on pages 20 and 38; Joy Davies of the Esperanto Association of Ireland for the photo on page 66; and Michelle Ashmore of the Ulster Museum Picture Library.

The writing of this book was made possible with the assistance of a bursary from An Chomairle Ealaíon/The Arts Council, for which I am grateful.

Early versions of some material in this book appeared in various journals. Thanks are due to Malachi O'Doherty, former editor of *Fortnight* magazine, and I am particularly grateful to Thomas Dillon Redshaw of *New Hibernia Review* for his thoughtful editorial input on the essay 'Tearmann: Sanctuary'. I am grateful to *Comhar* magazine's former editor Mícheál Ó hUanacháin for publishing the poems 'My Father's Dreams' and 'Mo Mháthair Sa Teach Banaltrais'.

Numerous people have encouraged me in the writing of this book, and I would like to give a heartfelt thanks to Louis de Paor, Tess Gallagher, Paula Meehan, Domhnall Mitchell and Nuala Ní Dhomhnaill. I am deeply grateful to Marsha Swan of Hag's Head Press for her faith in this project. Thanks to Siobán Devlin for help with proofing.

Thanks are due to Manus Carson, David Maybury and Kieran Nolan for their help in preparing images, and to Jim Berkeley for providing publicity photographs.

I am deeply grateful to my partner, Niamh Lawlor, for her support, and to our daughter Eithne for many laughs. A special thanks to Gerry Lawlor for looking after Eithne, and giving us time to concentrate on our work.

I would like to thank my family—sister Caitlín, brothers Ciaran, Pat and Breandán—for comments and help with photographs. I would like to thank my nephew Fionntán McElheran for his invaluable advice on the Irish language. Finally, this book would not exist but for my mother and father.

NOTES, SOURCES AND
FURTHER READING

The fairy tale *Na Trí Thonnaí* can be found in *Cogar san Fharraige*, edited by Proinsias Mac a' Bhaird (Coiscéim, 2002).

The contemporary account of the anti-Catholic and anti-socialist pogroms in Harland and Wolff was sourced in Jonathan Bardon's *Belfast: An Illustrated History* (Blackstaff Press, 1982).

Cathal Póirtéir's *Micí Sheáin Néill: scealaí agus scéalta* (Coiscéim, 1993) is an invaluable study of this storyteller's art.

Seosamh Mac Grianna's 'Galar na Gaeltachta' can be found in *Saothar Sheosaimh Mhic Grianna, Cuid a Dó: Ailt*, edited by Nollaig Mac Congáil (Coiste Foilsitheoireachta Chomhaltas Uladh, 1977). Fionntán de Brún's *Seosamh Mac Grianna: An Mhéin Rúin* (An Clóchomhar Tta, 2002) is an in-depth study of the writer's work. Pól Ó Muirí has written two biographies: *Seosamh Mac Grianna: Míreanna Saoil* (Cló Iar-Chonnachta, 2007) and *A Flight from Shadow: The Life and Work of Seosamh Mac Grianna* (Lagan Press, 1999).

The title of Mac Grianna's *Dá mBíodh Ruball ar an Éan* derives from the following Rann na Feirste storytelling trope, one that was often used by my father: *'Bhí sin ann agus is fada ó bhí. Dá mbéinn ann an t-am sin, ní bhéinn ann anois. Dá mbéinn bodhar ní chluinfinn é. Dá mbéinn dall ní fheicfinn é, 's dá mbíodh ruball ar an éan bheadh sé níos faide.'* (That was there and it's a long time since it was. If I were there that time, I wouldn't be here now. If I were deaf I wouldn't hear it. If I were blind, I wouldn't see it, and if there were a tail on the bird, it would be longer.)

For the stories of Oisín, Colm Cille and the Children of Lir, I referred to Dáithí Ó hÓgáin's *The Lore of Ireland: An Encyclopaedia of Myth, Legend and Romance* (Collins Press/Boydell Press, 2006).

A.T.Q. Stewart's *The Summer Soldiers: The 1798 Rebellion in Antrim and Down* (Blackstaff Press, 1995) provided much useful information about Henry Joy McCracken.

Heroes in the Wind: From Kull to Conan: The Best of Robert E. Howard, edited by John Clute (Penguin Classics, 2009) is the best introduction to Howard's work.

Gabrielle Maguire's *Our Own Language: An Irish Initiative* (Multilingual Matters, 1991) is a fascinating study of urban Irish speakers and bilingualism in Belfast.

The Cathal Ó Searcaigh line *'Caithfear pilleadh arís ar na foinsí'* comes from the poem 'An Tobar' ('The Well'), collected in *Homecoming/ An Bealach 'na Bhaile—Selected Poems/Rogha Dánta*, edited by Gabriel Fitzmaurice (Cló Iar-Chonnachta, 1993).

Padraic Ó Conaire's 'Aba-Cána-Lú' is in his classic short-story collection *An Chéad Chloch* (1914; reissued by Mercier Press, 1999).

The Michael Davitt line *'titeann an oíche gleann ar ghleann'* is from the poem 'Hiraeth', first published in *Gleann ar Ghleann* (Sáirséal/ Ó Marcaigh, 1981).

LIST OF ILLUSTRATIONS